# A Political Theology of the Bureaucratic State

# A Political Theology of the Bureaucratic State

## The Anonymous Sovereigns

Steven T. Lane

LEXINGTON BOOKS/FORTRESS ACADEMIC
*Lanham • Boulder • New York • London*

Published by Lexington Books/Fortress Academic
Lexington Books is an imprint of The Rowman & Littlefield Publishing Group, Inc.
4501 Forbes Boulevard, Suite 200, Lanham, Maryland 20706
www.rowman.com

86-90 Paul Street, London EC2A 4NE

Copyright © 2025 by The Rowman & Littlefield Publishing Group, Inc.

*All rights reserved.* No part of this book may be reproduced in any form or by any electronic or mechanical means, including information storage and retrieval systems, without written permission from the publisher, except by a reviewer who may quote passages in a review.

British Library Cataloguing in Publication Information Available

**Library of Congress Cataloging-in-Publication Data**

Names: Lane, Steven T., 1985- author.
Title: A political theology of the bureaucratic state : the anonymous sovereigns / Steven T. Lane.
Description: Lanham : Lexington Books, Fortress Academic, [2025] | Includes bibliographical references and index.
Identifiers: LCCN 2024036808 (print) | LCCN 2024036809 (ebook) | ISBN 9781978717046 (cloth ; alk. paper) | ISBN 9781978717053 (electronic)
Subjects: LCSH: Bureaucracy. | Christianity and politics.
Classification: LCC HM806 .L46 2024 (print) | LCC HM806 (ebook) | DDC 261.7–dc23/eng/20240910
LC record available at https://lccn.loc.gov/2024036808
LC ebook record available at https://lccn.loc.gov/2024036809

∞™ The paper used in this publication meets the minimum requirements of American National Standard for Information Sciences—Permanence of Paper for Printed Library Materials, ANSI/NISO Z39.48-1992.

*To Mandi, Isaac, Aiden, and Elijah*

# Contents

Acknowledgments ix

Introduction: The Irony of Political History 1

1 Toward a Typology of Sovereignty 13
2 Who Coerces the Coercers? 41
3 Who Shapes the Shapers? 59
4 Bureaucracy Ascendant 75
5 The Dominion of God 109
6 Resting from Coercion 137

Bibliography 151
Index 159
About the Author 161

# Acknowledgments

Anything worth considering in the following pages is due in large part to the community of support I have been fortunate to be with in the past decade. Thanks goes first and foremost to my advisor, John Kelsay, who helped me narrow down and focus my thinking as best he could. The rest of the Religion, Ethics, and Philosophy (REP) faculty—Matthew Day, Aline Kalbian, Martin Kavka, and the late, great Sumner Twiss, each pushed me to become a better scholar and teacher, but more so, a better person through their examples. Outside of REP, Adam Gaiser taught me the basics of the Islamic tradition (and taught my sons the basics of blowing straw wrappers at me). Michael McVicar was always ready to help and answer my questions, especially as issues of surveillance and material aspects of bureaucracy ebbed and flowed in my thinking. The friendships I have made here are equally important to my scholarship. My office compatriots over the years—John Cole, David Edwards, Thomas Greene, Rebeka Gordon, Sam Houston, and Michael McLaughlin—have been my social connection to the world in an otherwise solitary discipline. My appreciation also goes to the 2015 Religion Cohort for their friendship and support, and especially my fellow 2015 REP cohort—Luke Arrendando, Monique Colberg, and Nathan Moats were exactly the people I needed to travel with on this journey. My editor, Zach Nycum, has been a constant source of encouragement and assistance, as well as an anonymous peer-reviewer, whose comments were most helpful.

Lastly, I thank my family. To my mother for being my first and best teacher, my father for always listening to my off-the-wall ideas and helping to rein them back in, and to my sister for keeping me grounded. My children, Isaac, Aiden, and Elijah, are now all old enough to understand the intricacies of writing a book. But most importantly, to my wife Mandi, for being my better self; for being stronger, braver, and more loving than I could ever hope to be. None of this would have been possible without her patience and love.

# Introduction
## The Irony of Political History

The popular narrative of Anglo-European political development is well-developed and generally accepted. In rough outline—the monarchical systems of pre- and early modernity were displaced by self-sovereignty movements, idealized in the American and French Revolutions. The nineteenth century saw an exponential increase in the popular movements which would end colonialism and promote freedom. Other than the totalitarian hiccups of the twentieth century and the lingering power of certain theocratic regimes, history marches onward to the glories of freedom, autonomy, and self-determination.

My primary contention is that this history is not only flawed, but the truth is ultimately ironic as this narrative helps hide reality. Instead, I argue that the historical accident of bureaucratic systems, which were meant to serve the interests of freedom and autonomy, and the power vacuum of failure of liberal democracy have led to the iron cage of which Max Weber warned us. We are free in the same way a bird in a cage or a tiger in a zoo is free—given just enough freedom to believe we have it, while actually being constrained by forces beyond our power to control or, at times, recognize.

Before turning to the introduction, I will use the rest of this prologue to illustrate a minor version of this constrained freedom and gesture to the theoretical and practical issues that will be covered in later chapters.

### THIRD-PARTY CANDIDATES AND THE BINARY OF CHOICE

As of this writing, the 2024 election season has begun to ramp up to the fever pitch it will undoubtedly take. Beginning with the 2016 election, both major parties' candidates have had high unfavorable ratings across the political spectrum. The disillusionment stems in part from the brutal primaries of 2016 and the no less fraught Democratic primary of 2020 and Republican primary of 2024, respectively. Due to the polarization of American politics since the

Clinton era, primary voters (the base) are more partisan in outlook and are more likely to choose a similarly partisan candidate to be the nominee.[1]

Primary voters, then, seem to have a choice on their ballots, at least when their party is out of power. General election voters are constrained in their choices—one extreme or the other. The third-party candidacy of Robert Kennedy Jr. has disrupted the binary in a way not seen since Ross Perot in 1992, but it is unlikely he will receive a single electoral college vote. Why? The two-party system is designed to remain limited to only two parties. Ballot access, on a state-by-state approach, is one of the larger problems. However, the rhetoric around third-party candidates is more telling: spoiler candidate, throwing a vote away—these show the institutional disdain for other options, as if certain candidates were owed their turn or our votes.

Variations on this type of control reappear in the social safety net, the legal system, and the "free market" economic system. We have succumbed to the illusion of the zoo enclosure—not because it is safe, but because we are unable to imagine any other type of environment.

## THE TENSIONS OF CHRISTIAN POLITICAL THOUGHT

In his quasi-satirical account of the Christian life, *The Screwtape Letters*, C. S. Lewis observes the problem of evil that faces humanity in the modern world.

> The greatest evil is not now done in those sordid "dens of crime" that Dickens loved to paint. It is not done even in concentration camps and labour camps. In those we see its final result. But it is conceived and ordered (moved, seconded, carried, and minuted) in clean, carpeted, warmed, and well-lighted offices, by quiet men with white collars and cut fingernails and smooth-shaven cheeks who do not need to raise their voice. Hence, naturally enough, my symbol for Hell is something like the bureaucracy of a police state or the offices of a thoroughly nasty business concern.[2]

The horrors and tragedies of the twentieth century, from Auschwitz and the Soviet gulags to the killing fields of Cambodia, from the failure of the War on Poverty to the failure of the War on Drugs, can be traced back, in part, to a similar mindset or view of the world. The purpose of this work is to investigate and expose this mindset by focusing on concrete examples. To do so will require an interdisciplinary approach; however, the keystone will be Christian political thought.

The history of Western[3] political philosophy from the conversion of Constantine and the "Christianization" of Rome to the formation of modern nation-states in the aftermath of the Reformation of the sixteenth century was, in many ways, the history of the Church. As such, Western political theory, down to our contemporary moment, consists of attempts to reconcile the Platonic, the Christian, and the post-Christian philosophies and anthropologies of human reason, the purpose of politics, and the nature of humanity into a workable theory. The bulk of political philosophy has been a series of footnotes to *The Republic* and Romans 13.[4] During the past five centuries, Christian ethics and political theory have drifted further and further apart. Even though political theory had taken a turn away from Christian concepts before the bifurcation of religion/politics occurred under the guise of the Enlightenment in the early modern era as Europe fractured under the weight of the Catholic/Protestant split, the specter of Christianity still appears in the supposed secular space of political thought.

This book is not an attempt to construct a fully formed Christian political philosophy. A Christian political philosophy is impossible apart from beginning with the fundamentally theological claim "Christ is Lord." However, in an attempt to satisfy the Rawlsian consensus or to perform Public Theology (see below), many Western Christians have de-theologized the basis of their theological claims in the attempt to reach the masses. This leads to the unmooring of praxis and philosophy; "biblical," "family," or "traditional" *values* are extracted into an ahistorical frame of reference which is then applied back onto the political situations of contemporary life. Liberation Theology (also see below) swings the pendulum too far in the other direction in that it is over-contextualized and cannot be the basis of a larger Christian political philosophy.[5] A properly Christian political philosophy would require attention to the universal aspect of Christianity, while also contextualizing (or theologizing) the teachings for particular political types.

Instead, this work analyzes a particular point of contact between political theory and Christian ethics. That point is the locus of power, particularly *State* power, or sovereignty, in the form of coercion. The State-power-as-coercion formula is well established in most forms of political philosophy; the disagreements between scholars occur over the actualization of the coercive power. Unlike the premodern period where the coercive will of the sovereign could bear directly on subordinates, who would, in turn, apply coercive power on their own subordinates (an admittedly simplistic reading of what we call feudalism), the contemporary political structure is that of the bureaucracy, which acts as the will of the sovereign. It is my contention that bureaucratic regimes have assumed the functional role of sovereignty due to their ability to apply downward pressure on the individual citizen and the ability of bureaucracies to respond during a state of exception.

In American history alone, there are any number of examples of the coercive power of the bureaucracy as a tool of the sovereign.[6] Yet the fields of religious studies, Christian ethics, and political theology have not given this phenomenon the attention it deserves. I see two possible reasons for this lack. First, bureaucracy is not "sexy"—there is no immediate connection between the demands of justice and the bureaucratic state in the same manner as justice and minority rights or immigration. This is because of the second reason: a misunderstanding in the (particularly American) function of the bureaucrat or civil servant. Too often, the image of the bureaucrat is an overworked but un-caring DMV worker, who will still receive a paycheck whether the next person in line filled out the pink form or the green form, much less the correct form. This is due to the average citizens' interactions with the bureaucracy. Consider the following anecdote relayed by David Graeber:

> Kurt works for a subcontractor for the German military. Or . . . actually, he is employed by a subcontractor of a subcontractor of a subcontractor for the German military. Here is how he describes his work:
> The German military has a subcontractor that does their IT work.
> The IT firm has a subcontractor that does their logistics.
> The logistics firm has a subcontractor that does their personnel management, and I work for that company.
> Let's say soldier A moves to an office two rooms farther down the hall. Instead of just carrying his computer over there, he has to fill out a form.
> The IT subcontractor will get the form, people will read it and approve it, and forward it to the logistics firm.
> The logistics firm will then have to approve the moving down the hall and will request personnel from us.
> The office people in my company will then do whatever they do, and now I come in.
>
> I get an email: "Be at barracks B at time C." Usually these barracks are one hundred to five hundred kilometers [62–310 miles] away from my home, so I will get a rental car. I take the rental car, drive to the barracks, let dispatch know that I arrived, fill out a form, unhook the computer, load the computer into a box, seal the box, have a guy from the logistics firm carry the box to the next room, where I unseal the box, fill out another form, hook up the computer, call dispatch to tell them how long I took, get a couple of signatures, take my rental car back home, send dispatch a letter with all of the paperwork and then get paid.
>
> So instead of the soldier carrying his computer for five meters, two people drive for a combined six to ten hours, fill out around fifteen pages of paperwork, and waste a good four hundred euros of taxpayers' money.[7]

This story could be the dictionary definition of inefficient bureaucracy. However, it is also an example of bureaucracy for the sake of bureaucracy. One only needs to receive an audit notification from the Internal Revenue

Service to understand a different type of bureaucracy *and* a different form of coercion, which is the focus of this study. I seek to go one level further down than the obvious threat of an IRS audit, down to the point where bureaucratic systems can structure the very choices ostensibly "free" individuals are even able to make and fathom. There are, unfortunately, many examples of overt coercion/force meted out by State actors. The second half of the 2010s was marked by an increase (or, an increase in public awareness) of police misconduct, particularly on minority persons. On this issue, there are many, better qualified, scholars who have and are addressing such overt displays of power. Again, this study seeks to go below the overt problems (symptoms) and attempts to diagnose the disease.

Given these gaps in Christian ethical discourse, the question which motivates this work is as follows: What is the Christian ethical understanding of the asymmetrical, coercive power between the sovereign and the citizen as expressed through the domestic bureaucracy of modern liberal democracies? Reaching this answer will require a dissection of several important concepts: sovereignty, coercion, and bureaucracy. I will show that a Christian conception of sovereignty and coercion is compatible with a bureaucratic system, given that the bureaucratic system is placed under a rigorous system of checks-and-balances. It is my contention that such checks are not operating in most contexts and that Christian ethical reflection will provide a foundational level from which to critique, and possibly restructure such systems.

## THEORY AND METHOD

The field of religious studies is arguably the most interdisciplinary field in the modern academy. Methodological and theoretical insights run the gamut through the Humanities and Social Sciences while at the same time trying to navigate the historical, and at times, material connection to Theology. Even the STEM fields are brought into play with the constant debates over "religion and science," bioethics, and our increasing understanding of the human mind. Unfortunately, this apparent strength has its own kryptonite; religious studies, and religious ethics by extension, lacks a defined range of methodological choices. Whereas the respective social sciences have two to three major methodological schools which wax and wane over the generations, religious studies (as a field) relies on all methodological and theoretical schools across the disciplines.

Thus, this work is necessarily interdisciplinary and also lacks a social-science-adjacent methodology. We can arbitrarily justify any particular methodological approach, but what of the theoretical grounding which lies behind methodological considerations? I suggest the best way to analyze the concepts of this study is through the theoretical aspects of political theology. As a field of study, political theology is less than a half-century old; however, some aspects of political theology stretch back to at least Augustine, if not to the Pauline corpus of the New Testament. Political theology is best understood as an umbrella concept for more specialized interests in the study of the interaction between religion and politics.

Modern political theology was introduced by Carl Schmitt in his *Political Theology: Four Chapters on the Concept of Sovereignty*,[8] in response to the prevailing neo-Kantian conceptions of political systems that were dominant in Germany in the inter-war period. Political theology begins with the notion that

> All significant concepts of the modern theory of the state are secularized theological concepts not only because of their historical development—in which they were transferred from theology to the theory of the state, whereby, for example, the omnipotent god became the omnipotent lawgiver—but also because of their systematic structure, the recognition of which is necessary for a sociological consideration of these concepts.[9]

From these two concepts, secularization and systematic similarities, political theology has expanded into several areas. The following is an overview of the state of the field of political theology and an attempt to solidify a conceptual understanding for the purpose of this study.

Elizabeth Phillips[10] lays out a tripartite conception of political theology: Political Theology,[11] Public Theology, and Liberation Theology. These categories are structured around their respective purposes but also take on a geographical element.[12] Political Theology is grounded in European post-Holocaust theology, represented by thinkers such as Metz, Moltmann, and Sölle. Public Theology is a North American phenomenon, driven by the issues of Church-State separation, with the attendant need of speaking non-theologically in the public square (Tracy and Stackhouse) and at times challenging the rules of the dominant secular playbook (Neuhaus). Liberation Theology, in its original form, is a product of the various political, social, and ideological forces at work in Latin and South America, represented by Gutiérrez and Boff. Liberation theology has expanded into identity-grounded theologies of various types.

Peter Scott and William T. Cavanaugh lay out three differing possibilities for political theology, all of which could be simultaneously descriptive of the field. The first option is a sharp division between religion and politics:

> For some, politics is seen as a "given" with its own secular autonomy. Politics and theology are therefore two essentially distinct activities, one to do with

public authority, and the other to do in the first place with religious experience and the semiprivate associations of religious believers. The task of political theology might be to relate religious belief to larger societal issues while not confusing the proper autonomy of each.[13]

Michael Kirwan, commenting on this passage, notes that this is a "render unto Caesar" approach to religion and politics: "Each has their 'proper autonomy'; if this autonomy is infringed then both sides suffer."[14] Luther remains the clearest proponent of this approach; however, most contemporary Christian traditions argue that the autonomy of the political sphere is judged by theological claims of justice and rightness.

The second possibility, according to Scott and Cavanaugh, is that

> theology is critical reflection on the political. Theology is related as superstructure to the material politico-economic base. Theology reflects and reinforces just or unjust political arrangements. The task of political theology might then be to expose the ways in which theological discourse reproduces inequalities of class, gender or race, and to reconstruct theology so that it serves the cause of justice.[15]

This approach seems to capture modern Liberation Theology. Liberation Theology is radically normative (as opposed to the other two options), as its descriptive work ends at the point of proving the oppression of a particular group in need of liberation.

The third and final option is an interpretation of Schmitt's claim:

> For still others, theology and politics are essentially similar activities; both are constituted in the production of metaphysical images around which communities are organized. All politics has theology embedded within it, and particular forms of organization are implicit in doctrines of, for example, Trinity, the church and eschatology. There is no essential separation of material base and cultural superstructure. The task then might become one of exposing the false theologies underlying supposedly "secular" politics and promoting the true politics implicit in a true theology.[16]

This approach (which seems to be the one Scott and Cavanaugh favor) seems to synthesize all three of Phillips's categories: Metz focuses on Ecclesiology, Moltmann on Eschatology; liberation theologies focus on the plight of the oppressed and God's liberating action in history; and Public Theology seeks to uncover the "religious" reality behind the "secular" veneer of politics.

The history and effects of the secularization of theological terms into politics are the keys to understanding political theology as a theory. To an extent, historians of various stripes have been describing the key Schmittian claim for the past two centuries. Any history or genealogy that interacts with the historical process of the "secularization" of Europe is participating in the widest and most descriptive forms of political theology. As a brief explanation, I will introduce a basic aspect of sovereignty before turning to more complex forms in chapter 1.

The Abrahamic traditions assert that sovereignty belongs to God, not only in that he is the creator, but that he is understood to be all-knowing and all-powerful.[17] Thus, the will of God is (nearly[18]) unlimited. If sovereignty is secularized and applied to the State (either in the form of a monarch or a bureaucratic system), sovereignty is no longer the prerogative of an all-knowing and all-powerful being. In theory, the king is all-powerful in his realm, in so far as human power is concerned, and in so far as he can actually gather the resources to enforce his will. However, the king is never all-knowing, no matter what theoretical system is put in place to represent the king. The king can declare a new set of taxes, but it falls to those further down the pecking order to enforce that will. In addition, the king cannot always know that his will is being carried out. An unhappy nobleman could fluster the king's sovereignty and the king may never discover it. The example remains the same if we update the political system to representative democracies. Clearly, human sovereignty means something different than God's sovereignty. Because the subject of the sovereign has changed, the meaning of that power has also changed—God's sovereignty must mean something different than the sovereignty expressed or claimed by any temporal, finite State. Alasdair MacIntyre makes a similar argument regarding the entire field of ethics.[19] I am not suggesting that we should go to a similar extreme in the field of theo-political thought. However, I do think we should approach political terminology in similar ways as MacIntyre does ethics, albeit more modest and constrained. If theo-political words have changed meaning, we can trace the process of secularization, which would help us make sense of the "why" and "how."

## POLITICAL THEOLOGY AS ETHICS

Regardless of any changes in meaning, it is clear that political theology functions as an ethical discourse, just as political philosophy. Ethical questions (what should one do?) can only be answered after the anthropological question (what is a person?[20]) has been exposed as an implicit question in all ethical deliberations. Political theories answer the anthropological question with actions: *homo politicus*, *homo economicus*, *homo faber*, etc., each with a variety of more specific neologisms. Humans are "doers" and "actors"; meaning is found in the doing and acting. By contrast (or at the least, in addition), the Christian tradition grounds humanity in the *imago dei*; even with a multitude of possible interpretations of the phrase, the *imago dei* must mean that humans and God share in *something*. In the Christian tradition, the anthropological question is answered by the divine; meaning is found in relation to God. Political theology helps to bridge this apparent gap between the political and theological by exploring the political manifestations of the *imago dei*. Christian ethics adds an intermediate step between the anthropological assumption and the ethical question: the theo-political grounding of Christian ethics as a system of thought. Political theology as Christian ethics asks questions along the lines of "How does the *imago dei* do the work of *homo politicus*?" The question "what now?" (an inherently ethical question) rises in response to the "why?" and "how?" As an ethical discourse, political theology can lead to constructive developments in the contemporary political context by opening a deeper, more fundamental line of give-and-take reasoning.

A brief explanation of my use of *tradition* seems appropriate at this point. I will follow Alasdair MacIntyre's definition of tradition:

> A tradition is an argument extended through time in which certain fundamental agreements are defined and redefined in terms of two kinds of conflict: those with critics and enemies external to the tradition who reject all or at least key parts of those fundamental agreements, and those internal, interpretative debates through which the meaning and rationale of the fundamental agreements come to be expressed and by whose progress a tradition is constituted. Such internal debates may on occasion destroy what had been the basis of common fundamental agreement, so that either a tradition divides into two or more warring components, whose adherents are transformed into external critics of each other's positions, or else the tradition loses all coherence and fails to survive. It can also happen that two traditions, hitherto independent and even antagonistic, can come to recognize certain possibilities of fundamental agreement and reconstitute themselves as a single, more complex debate.[21]

This study concerns at least two traditions: modern liberalism and Christianity, which seem to have progressed together through most of the stages MacIntyre notes. This study asks a different set of questions—or asks them in a different way than previous studies. My model for this type of question comes from Oliver O'Donovan's *The Desire of the Nations*. In critiquing the "Northern school" (O'Donovan's shorthand for what Phillips calls Political Theology), he asks a series of questions:

> The questions that confront the Northern democracies require detailed attention to the structures of authority which undergird their unruly democratic culture: can democracy avoid corruption by mass communication? Can individual liberty be protected from technological manipulation? Can Civil

rights be safeguarded without surrendering democratic control to arbitrarily appointed courts? Or stable market-conditions without surrendering control to arbitrarily appointed bankers? Can punishment be humane and still satisfy the social conscience? Can international justice be protected by threats of nuclear devastation? Can ethnic, cultural and linguistic communities assert their identities without opposing individual freedoms? Can democracy contain the urge to excessive consumption of natural resources? Can the handicapped, the elderly and the unborn be protected against the exercise of liberty demanded by the strong, the articulate and the middle aged? Should the nation state yield place to a large, market-defined governmental conglomerates? These are the questions that political theology, in its self-conscious forms, is the most notable for never addressing.[22]

These are the type of questions within the modern liberal traditions which should be answerable from the Christian ethical tradition. Even though these questions are presented rhetorically in a yes/no binary, they call for deep and subtle explorations before turning to any policy solutions to the problems they raise. Adding the question "how?" moves political theology beyond the abstract, into a space I will call *practical political theology*.

## CHAPTER OUTLINES

Chapter 1 focuses on the nature of sovereignty as a concept in political theology. I trace the history of sovereignty from Hobbes through the French Revolution (and defend the choice of this time period). I then turn to a modified version of Weber's *Herrschaft*, or sociology of lordship,[23] in order to update it to the contemporary political moment.

Chapter 2 continues with Weber, building a framework for understanding and interpreting the bureaucratic systems which make up most of the modern liberal political order. I argue that sovereignty cannot be held by "the people" nor the politicians who are voted in and out of office. Instead, it is the bureaucratic class that holds a position of sovereignty.

Chapter 3 turns to tools or methods through which sovereignty is transferred from the sovereign, through the bureaucrats, to the individual. This tool is coercion, an underdeveloped concept in Christian ethics, both in itself and as a part of domestic political arrangements.

Chapter 4 is a three-part case study on the nature of coercive bureaucracies, drawing together gender, race, and public health as special points of contact between individuals and the coercive bureaucratic state.

Chapter 5 brings the resources of the Christian ethical tradition to bear on the problem of coercive sovereignty. Through a combination of biblical and theological sources, I show that coercion appears to be a necessary part of the human condition in a world affected by sin. However, given that coercion can also become sinful, it is necessary to seek guiderails, whether explicit or implicit, within the Christian tradition to show the boundaries of coercive power.

Finally, chapter 6 engages a possible response from within the Christian tradition to the power of coercive bureaucracies and the problems they cause.

## NOTES

1. The exception to this rule, and perhaps helping to prove it, is the Democratic National Committee's decision to not require a primary in 2024, allowing some states to grant their delegates directly to Biden. In both parties, the base and establishment are often at odds—see the 2016 primaries.

2. In the preface to the 1961 Edition of C. S. Lewis, *The Screwtape Letters*, Annotated ed. (New York: HarperCollins, 2013), xxxvii.

3. Edward Said has illustrated the constructed nature of the Occidental/Oriental divide, calling into question the use of "West." As no better term seems to exist, I will follow Marcel Gauchet, who, in commenting on similar terms, argued, "I feel it is better to adopt consciously a tradition that is open to criticism than to attempt to surpass it by conjuring up a new term." Marcel Gauchet, *The Disenchantment of the World: A Political History of Religion*, trans. Oscar Burge (Princeton, NJ: Princeton University Press, 1997), 8. The same can be said of gendered nouns (man, mankind) in quotations. On Said, see *Orientalism* (New York: Random House, 1978).

4. This is an allusion to Alfred N. Whitehead's comment, "The safest general characterization of the European philosophical tradition is that it consists of a series of footnotes to Plato," Alfred North Whitehead, *Process and Reality: An Essay in Cosmology*, ed. David Ray Griffin and Donald W. Sherburne (New York: Free Press, 1978), 39.

5. This is seen most clearly in the various identity theologies (black, feminist, LGBT, etc.) which, in their hyper-specificity, have necessitated sub-theologies (womanist, latinx, etc.). While these are fascinating and important theological traditions, the universality of the Christian message (a fundamental claim of the tradition) is the proverbial forest that is lost because of the trees.

6. The nature of supranational sovereignty, currently best expressed through the European Union, is a slightly more complex phenomenon. While I will make occasional references to the UK, these should be understood as part of the Anglo-American tradition.

7. David Graeber, *Bullshit Jobs: A Theory* (New York: Simon & Schuster, 2019), 14, paragraph breaks original. Thanks goes to Matt Day for pointing me to this source.

8. Carl Schmitt, *Political Theology: Four Chapters on the Concept of Sovereignty*, trans. George Schwab (Cambridge, MA: The MIT Press, 1985). Hereinafter *PT*. For the controversy surrounding Schmitt, see chapter 2.

9. Ibid., 36.

10. Elizabeth Phillips, *Political Theology: A Guide for the Perplexed* (New York: T&T Clark, 2012), 42ff. The rest of this paragraph is heavily influenced by Phillips's breakdown of the categories.

11. I will follow Phillips in using the lowercase "political theology" to discuss the broader field and the uppercase "Political Theology" as a specific subset of that field.

12. O'Donovan fully embraces the geographic understanding, referring to a northern school and implying a southern school. See Oliver O'Donovan, *The Desire of the Nations* (New York: Cambridge University Press, 1996), 3.

13. Peter Scott and William T. Cavanaugh, "Introduction," in *The Blackwell Companion to Political Theology*, ed. William T. Cavanaugh and Peter Scott (Malden, MA: Blackwell Publishing, 2004), 2.

14. Michael Kirwan, *Political Theology: A New Introduction* (London: Darton, Longman and Todd, 2008), 5.

15. Scott and Cavanaugh, 2.

16. Ibid.

17. The overwhelming majority of adherents in the Abrahamic traditions use the masculine pronoun for God, while also asserting that God is beyond the finitude of gender. I have consciously chosen to be consistent with the sources I am using in this study; also, see footnote 4 above.

18. The debate in Christian theology in regards to God's omnipotence is fiercely contested. Does God will things because they have a goodness in themselves, or are certain things good because God wills them? Both options are fraught will pitfalls, the first posits a Platonic-like "good" existing apart from God (does this external good measure God's goodness?), while the second suggests that God could have willed humans to steal candy from babies (could God have willed things that we consider to be immoral?). The Euthyphro Problem still troubles monotheisms.

19. Alasdair MacIntyre, *After Virtue*, 2nd ed. (Notre Dame, IN: Notre Dame University Press, 1984).

20. This is another, perhaps less controversial way, of getting at "human nature."

21. Alasdair MacIntyre, *Whose Justice? Which Rationality?* (Notre Dame, IN: Notre Dame University Press, 1988), 12.

22. O'Donovan, 18.

23. *Herrschaft* is usually translated as "dominion" but as John Kelsay mentioned to me in a conversation, this hides the aspect of legitimacy inherent in the term. "Lordship" is not commonplace in the modern world, but it is a more accurate translation.

# 1

# Toward a Typology of Sovereignty

**I** begin this chapter by unpacking the theories of sovereignty expressed in Weber and Schmitt. I argue that we must take Schmitt's critiques of democratic systems seriously, especially in the way his theory undermines the notion of "the sovereignty of the People." I then return to Hobbes and Locke to consider the development of social contract systems. I posit that Schmitt's Hobbesianism and desire for a stronger unitary government stem from their respective historical positions. I also show that Hobbes's theory is closer to historic realities than Locke's. Finally, I return to the theoretical and develop my own typology of sovereignty, which pulls together the various strands of this chapter: political philosophy, political theology, and sociology. Altogether, this chapter seeks to conceptualize sovereignty and displace it from its traditional locus in contemporary political thought.

## WEBER AND SCHMITT

I have chosen to start with Max Weber due to his methodology. Weber gathers diverse evidence, formulates the ideal type from the evidence, then reapplies the ideal-type to the evidence, with the understanding that the ideal-type is the synthesis of data, and thus will not be replicated in reality. Through this back-and-forth of evidence and ideal-type, Weber is a model of the intellectual humility and creativity needed for complex interpretive debates.

Weber is rightly considered one of the fathers of modern sociology for his focus on the factors of the modern state. His life spanned Bismarck, Wilhelm, the Great War, and the Weimar Republic, dying before the terror of the Nazis was at hand.[1] The final four hundred pages of Weber's posthumous *Economy and Society* are devoted to the questions of political power: what systems exist(ed) to actualize the authority of the political rulers? Weber discerns three broad systems in history—personal authority expressed in either tradition or charisma and the institutionalized/bureaucratic. Weber defines tradition as "that which is customary and has always been so and prescribes obedience to some particular person."[2] In "Politics as a Vocation," he refers to the same authority as "custom" or "the authority of the 'eternal yesterday.'"[3] The divine right of kings, a rule proved more by the exceptions (and executions) of Charles II and Louis XVI, fits this understanding. The throne is the symbol to which the populace is loyal, thus the call of the crier, "The king is dead! Long live the king!" Charisma is also a species of personal authority, but the symbol is overridden by the person. This is "the surrender to the extraordinary, the belief in *charisma*, i.e., actual revelation or grace resting in such a person as a savior, a prophet, or a hero."[4] The charismatic leader can dispose of the symbols of loyalty due to the subjective view of her followers that she is "appointed," "called," or "destined" either by a divine force or the unavoidable march of history. The quintessential charismatic leader can quickly dissolve into an authoritarian system; both Julius Caesar and Adolf Hitler were "heroes" to their respective populaces and thus were able to undo the systems which had made up their former political systems.

Both tradition and charisma are contrasted with the rationalized bureaucratic system, which functions under formalized and general rules. These rules are developed with a goal in mind, efficiency being one of the most important for Weber in the development of the modern state. Personal authority is localized both for the traditional and charismatic systems. Any number of factors could affect the decision-making of the singular authority. The end of the action can be lost in the emotions, biases, or other non-rational aspects of life. The rule-based decision-making of the bureaucrat is a check against these non-rational aspects. The bureaucrat does not judge, that is, make decisions; instead, she implements decisions made further up the hierarchy of the bureaucracy. Thus, the most interesting part of the bureaucracy is where the line between decision-making and implementation is blurred (which we will turn to in chapter 3). The top of the bureaucracy is the source of the rules which govern the actions of the entire bureaucracy. I will return to Weber frequently, but for now, the key aspect of his thought is the move from the irrational to the rational as an aspect of society/culture/worldview.

The problem of sovereignty in the Weimar Republic was acute beyond the political problems of hyperinflation, massive unemployment, and the psychological depression of military defeat. Schmitt's *Political Theology: Four Chapters on Sovereignty* is a response to the gap he detects in the Weimar Constitution and, by extension, certain neo-Kantian jurists who did not see the same flaws. Schmitt is a controversial and complicated figure which his historical context does little to mitigate. Schmitt's legal career spanned the

Wilhelm, Weimar, and Third Reich forms of German history. He joined the National Socialists in 1933 after Hitler was granted emergency power by the *Reichstag*. This has led to the occasional, but I believe misguided, charge of opportunism. Instead, I see Schmitt as latching onto the closest thing he believed could save the constitutional order of the Weimar Republic. A key piece of evidence in this regard comes from Hannah Arendt. Hidden away in a footnote on intellectuals who supported Hitler, she suggests that Schmitt was not a "proper" Nazi: "as early as the middle thirties, [Schmitt] was replaced by the Nazi's *own brand* of political and legal theorists."[5] I suggest this is due to his outsider status; Schmitt never fit into the larger totalitarian system, as Arendt describes it, because he still held on to the "older" political models of state sovereignty and the friend/enemy distinction. While we may be (rightly) uncomfortable with his constructive program of legal and political thought, Schmitt's descriptive and critical work is too important to be assigned to the dustbin of history. Today, Schmitt is best utilized as an observer and polemicist, not a theory builder.[6]

In *Political Theology*, Schmitt is responding to the positivism of the prevailing neo-Kantian legal theory of his day while also interacting with the theories of his onetime teacher Weber. We return to Schmitt's famous dictum in full:

> All significant concepts of the modern theory of the state are secularized theological concepts not only because of their historical development—in which they were transferred from theology to the theory of the state, whereby, for example, the omnipotent god became the omnipotent lawgiver—but also because of their systematic structure, the recognition of which is necessary for a sociological consideration of these concepts.[7]

Schmitt suggests a different type of development than Weber. The irrational/rational divide in Weber exists in Schmitt as a change in the locus of power. The "death" of God does not mean the destruction of the divine attributes. Instead, they are appropriated by the new political prophets and founding heroes. This is most clear from the history of France between the Revolution and the final defeat of Napoleon. The Rights of Man replaced the Decalogue, the cultic apparatus of the Catholic Church was replaced by the Cult of Reason, "faith, hope, and love" by *liberté, égalité, fraternité*.[8] Foucault's panopticon (to which I return in chapter 3) is the State's omniscience, to say nothing of the civil religion envisioned by Rousseau which served to ground morality in something other than the divine. Schmitt's formulation is the transition from religion to philosophy to "the instrumental rationality of technical reason, mathematics, and the natural sciences."[9]

None of the preceding shows a real difference between Weber and Schmitt. Various scholars have linked Weber and Schmitt in the past; Wolfgang Mommsen in the 1950s and the comments of Jürgen Habermas in 1964 ("legitimate pupil" and "natural son").[10] The difference between Weber and Schmitt lies in their view of the transition. If rationality undermines the idea of an omnipotent god, it also generates the conditions for the development of the omnipotent lawgiver. Even the deism of the eighteenth century had a place for eternal judgment.[11] As the role of Christianity declined in the public sphere as part of the move to rationality, the threat of divine punishment went with it. Darwin, or more appropriately the social Darwinists of the nineteenth century, had shown the superiority of humanity in the world of the natural; if the supernatural was removed, then humanity was superior above all things. The rejection of sin and human frailty quickly followed the rejection of heaven and hell. The omnipotent (rational, scientific) lawgiver was a valid option in the utopian projects of the time.

Of course, by Schmitt's time, the idealistic optimism of the late nineteenth century had been replaced by the brutal reality of the Great War. This brings us back to the problem of sovereignty in the Weimar Republic. Schmitt's other famous dictum, "Sovereign is he who decides the exception," is based originally on the power of God to perform a miracle. If God chooses to violate the natural order (Hume), he may do so on the grounds of his own sovereignty. The exception is any event that the law is unable to face due to its limitations as a human creation. If the law could provide guidance in the exception, it would not be an exceptional moment, just as divine healing is unnecessary when the medical intervention is successful. The exception, as its name entails, is just as rare as the miracle. The sovereign is the one who straddles the limits of the law. When the law is able to deal with the situations at hand, the sovereign is bound by it like any other person. However, when the law fails, and the exception arises, the sovereign is elevated by the demands of the moment to transcend the law.

This is also the source of much of Schmitt's critique of liberalism. "The people" cannot be sovereign under Schmitt's definition. A plebiscite for a democracy any larger than the Greek city-states (recalling that only a tiny fraction of the population was qualified as citizens) is inefficient to respond to the type of emergency that the exception represents. The republican system of representation is better suited to handle emergencies (the United States has 535 members of Congress, while the UK's House of Commons has 650 members[12]), but this still does not give sovereignty to "the People," nor can it stand in as the "will of the People." A more apt phrase would be the "will of the majority." Any type of body must be led by a singular will or be impaired; Abraham Lincoln's famous line (paraphrasing Jesus) "A house divided will not stand." While not to level of division as Lincoln witnessed, recent elections are clear examples of the division within the will of the People. The electoral votes for Michigan were decided by 0.3 percent in 2016[13] and the 2018 Florida Senate race by 0.1 percent of the votes.[14] "We the people" may have been unified in their opposition to British tyranny, but contemporary examples are few and far between.

Schmitt's situation in Weimar was exponentially worse. The Anglo-American system has, for better or worse, had small numbers of functional political parties.[15] The continental experience is one of a multiplicity of political parties, perhaps best illustrated by Schmitt's Weimar. The need for a plurality victor created the opening through which Hitler came into power. Schmitt's critique of democratic systems is based on his own historical moment and cultural milieu, just as any critique is.

The ultimate comparison of Weber and Schmitt depends on how one views the move to rationality. It is clear that Schmitt is critical of the rationalization of the world. If Weber is understood as optimistic about the rational order of modernity, then Habermas's claim needs to be updated. However, if Weber is interpreted pessimistically,[16] that the inevitability of the iron cage is something to be feared, not celebrated, then the two are more alike on this issue than is normally granted. They are different, however, in how they view traditional religious concepts to be operating in the modern world. Agamben notes:

> Schmitt's strategy is, in a certain sense, the opposite of Weber's. While, for Weber, secularization was an aspect of the growing process of disenchantment and detheologization of the modern world, for Schmitt it shows on the contrary that, in modernity, theology continues to be present and active in an eminent way. This does not necessarily imply an identity of substance between theology and modernity, or a perfect identity of meaning between theological and political concepts, rather it concerns a particular strategic relation that marks political concepts and refers them back to their theological origin.[17]

According to Schmitt, theology is the specter that haunts modernity. Modernity is based on the rejection of Christian theology and is only coherent insofar as theology is still available as a foil. The full process of secularization, in the form of ridding theology and religion as possible systems of thought, would result in the destruction of modernity as its own system of thought. As an analogy, the early Protestant Reformers required Catholicism in order to *protest* against it and to *reform* the Church. Without the Catholic background, Protestantism loses part of its meaning. It may be possible that Protestant theology could (as an outworking of MacIntyre's concept of tradition) exist apart from Catholicism. Likewise, without the Christian theological background, modernity loses part of its meaning. It is less clear that modernity could continue as a tradition without the constant threat of a return to pre-modern theological systems. For Schmitt, secularization cannot claim victory because of the theology hiding in its own necessity.[18]

To summarize to the Schmitt/Weber comparison, Schmitt's definition of sovereignty calls for a unified will, acting in situations for which the legislature did not prepare a legal framework. Weber's *charismatic* ideal-type leader functions similarly but through force of will. With this understanding of sovereignty, we can turn to the history of modern political philosophy.

## HOBBES

Machiavelli is often the reference point for the opening of political modernity, but this strikes me as a misunderstanding of Machiavelli's works. He understands the powers-that-be as historical realities who need tactical guidance on how to best do their jobs. Machiavelli is the first modern political scientist, but Thomas Hobbes has the claim to being the first modern political philosopher. Hobbes also represents the beginning of the social contract theory in political philosophy. Before turning to Hobbes, I will begin by sketching out the background from which Hobbes developed his ideas.

The medieval world was made up of overlapping and at times contradictory allegiances and loyalties. One was loyal to the Church, and to the Crown, and to one's city, and to one's guild. The story of medieval Europe could be traced in terms of the conflicts between these four spheres: the constant struggle between the papacy and monarchs, the power of the guilds and the cities against the centralizing power of the monarch, even the occasional skirmish between the Pope and a monastic order. The problems with such conflicting loyalties were clear to thinkers of the day. The solution was undivided loyalty. The Reformation shattered the only force that could have garnered such loyalty. The doctrine of *cuius regio, eius religio* and the Peace of Westphalia elevated the monarchy to the position of sovereign.[19] It also reinforced a system where physical control of territory in terms of borders and maps became the primary measure of sovereignty. The interplay between Event and Idea, or to put it another way, the tension between historical contingency and philosophical abstraction, needed explication in terms of the new reality of sovereign power.

The intellectual history of sovereignty as a matter of modern political concern originates with Jean Bodin, but his thought, much like Erasmus and Machiavelli in other contexts, straddles the line between the medieval and the modern to such a strong degree that it is difficult to properly place his thinking.²⁰ The first fully modern political thinker on the issue of sovereignty was Thomas Hobbes. "The modern state . . . is an inverted pyramid, its apex resting upon the 1651 folio edition of Hobbes's *Leviathan*."²¹ Much like Plato for the pre-modern world, Hobbes sets contours for a modern political philosophy which have, to date, not been erased.

Hobbes's political philosophy is a response to a growing set of concerns going back to at least the conflict between Henry VIII and Thomas More over papal primacy in the lead-up to the English Reformation. The conflict between the Stuart line and the English Parliament resulted in a series of civil wars, ultimately ending in the regicide of Charles I and the banishment of Charles II. This conflict is critical for understanding Hobbes.

> Before the reign of James I, it was widely accepted that England had a mixed constitution. . . . It could be used to defend the rights of Parliament against the Crown; but it certainly did not preclude a major, and in some versions even a dominant, role for the king, as long as it was understood that all rule was ultimately subject to the law as promulgated by the "Crown in Parliament", which mean the monarch together with the two houses of Parliament.²²

While James I was able to maintain a relationship with Parliament, though he coined the term "divine right of kings,"²³ his son, Charles I, was less than successful. From 1629 to 1640, Charles I did not convene Parliament, given his conflicts with it in the early 1620s.²⁴ It is in this context that Hobbes begins writing. Hobbes's *De cive* was published in 1642 and *Leviathan* in 1651.²⁵ Sabine positions Hobbes within the Royalist camp but also notes that no matter what Hobbes's motivations for writing *Leviathan*, "His political philosophy had too wide a sweep to make good propaganda."²⁶

As with any political theorist before the nineteenth century, one must work to understand the political theory apart from any now out-of-date scientific claims about humanity and nature. For Hobbes, this notion is one of "mechanical causation."²⁷ According to Sabine, Hobbes's view was that

> every event is a motion all sorts of natural processes must be explained by analysing complex appearances into the underlying motions of which they consist. . . . Thus he conceived the project of a system of philosophy in three parts, the first dealing with body and including what would now be called geometry and mechanics (or physics), the second including the physiology and psychology of individual human beings, and the third concluding with the most complex of all bodies, the "artificial" body called society or the state.²⁸

Thus, while Hobbes is (rightly) viewed as a monarchist, his philosophy works its way up, not down as most monarchical systems do. As Hobbes states:

> NATURE (the Art whereby God hath made and governes the World) is by the *Art* of man, as in many other things, so in this also imitated, that it can make an Artificiall Animal. For what is the *Heart*, but a *Spring*; and the *Nerves*, but so many *Strings*; and the *Ioynts*, but so many *Wheeles*, giving motion to the whole Body, such as was intended by the Artificer? *Art* goes yet further, imitating that Rationall and most excellent worke of Nature, *Man*. For by Art is created that great LEVIATHAN called a COMMON-WEALTH, or STATE, (in latine CIVITAS) which is but an Artificiall Man; though of greater stature and strength than the Naturall, for whose protection and defence it was intended; and in which, the *Soveraignty* is an Artificiall *Soul*, as giving life and motion to the whole body.[29]

The sovereignty of a political body is its soul, which, like a human soul, is unified (Plato's tripartite division of the soul was replaced by the Cartesian body/soul dualism, a marker in philosophy for the Modern period).

One of the important aspects that can be detached from Hobbes's motion-centric philosophy is his understanding of humans in relationships. Humans are equal in so far as they are not so different "that one man can thereupon claim to himselfe any benefit, to which another may not pretend, as well as he."[30] This equality in humanity is necessary for Hobbes's most famous argument:

> From this equality of ability, ariseth equality of hope in the attaining of our Ends. And therefore if any two men desire the same thing, which neverthelesse they cannot both enjoy, they become enemies; and in the way to their End, (which is principally their owne conservation, and sometimes their delectation only,) endeavour to destroy, or subdue one another.[31]

Hobbes's state of nature is often understood as being historically rooted, that is, humans before civilization were as Hobbes describes. While this may be accurate, it does not cover all of Hobbes's understandings of the state of nature. A better understanding of Hobbes is that the state of nature is always lurking, waiting for the defenses of civilization (or the Leviathan, see below) to fall. Humanity unconstrained by the protections of civilization will descend into the state of nature because it is *natural*. This is Hobbes the pessimistic realist, influenced by his own historical experiences. The natural world, apart from the coercive aspects of civilization, is one based on competition of scarce resources, and this competition is dangerous for all involved. Hobbes goes so far as to call this state of nature "war," which "is of every man, against every man."[32] This is the existence that is "solitary, poore, nasty, brutish, and short."[33] More so:

> To this warre of every man against every man, this also is consequent; that nothing can be Unjust. The notions of Right and Wrong, Justice and Injustice

have there no place. Where there is no common Power, there is no Law: where no Law, no Injustice. Force, and Fraud, are in warre the two Cardinall vertues. Justice and Injustice are none of the Faculties neither of the Body, nor Mind. If they were, they might be in a man that were alone in the world, as well as his Senses, and Passions. They are Qualities, that relate to men in Society, not in Solitude.[34]

In a move that reminds one of the more contemporary positivist legal tradition, Hobbes elevates the body which promulgates the law as the basis of justice. Without such a body (whether an individual or group), justice is an empty notion. Hobbes is unable to explain this state without falling back onto the moral language of "Force and Fraud." Force is (generally) morally neutral, but fraud is a form of deception. If justice (giving to each her due) does not exist in such a state, then fraud cannot exist either, because no one has anything due to them. Though there is no justice, there are rights, or more appropriately, a specific right:

> The RIGHT OF NATURE, which Writers commonly call *Jus Naturale*, is the Liberty each man hath, to use his own power, as he will himselfe, for the preservation of his own Nature; that is to say, of his own Life; and consequently, of doing any thing, which in his own Judgement, and Reason, hee shall conceive to be the aptest means thereunto.[35]

The ethically correct decision is the one which increases one's chance of survival. Fraud, thus, is not "immoral." Instead, it is a tool that is useful in some circumstances but less useful in others. Hobbes's ethic, at least at this point in its development, is entirely consequentialist and egoistic. Liberty, for Hobbes, is "the absence of externall Impediments" and is understood as a natural right.[36] The *Lex Naturalis*, or natural law,

> is a Precept, or general Rule, found out by Reason by which a man is forbidden to do, that, which is destructive of his life, or taketh away the means of preserving the same; and to omit, that by which he thinketh it may be best preserved.[37]

Hobbes reduces the natural law theory of Aquinas to the first principle: survival. Liberty plus survival leads Hobbes to the first two laws of nature:

> *That every man, ought to endeavor Peace, as farre as he has hope of obtaining it; and when he cannot obtain it, that he may seek, and use, all helps, and advantages of Warre. . . . That a man be willing, when others are so too, as farre-forth, as for Peace, and defence of himselfe he shall think it necessary, to lay down this right to all things; and be contented with so much liberty against other men, as he would allow other men against himselfe* (emphasis in original).[38]

Peace is valuable insofar as it leads to one's safety and security. If "peace" is threatening that safety, then "war" is the correct option. To summarize: Hobbes sets out a state of nature in which all humans are at war with one another for scarce, non-sharable goods, especially but not limited to the goods needed for survival. Reason, as a law of nature, indicates that humans should seek peace when possible to prolong their own survival. For the sake of peace, humans should "lay down" certain rights, which Hobbes goes on to explain as either renunciation or transference.[39] Transference of a right to someone leads to a contract.[40] Contracts, or covenants (Hobbes uses the latter in regards to future actions by one party[41]), create one of the conditions for justice. Yet for Hobbes, there is a deeper condition for justice, the possibility of injustice. Injustice, the breaking of a contract or covenant,[42] requires the possibility of punishment for the injustice committed.

> Therefore before the names of Just, and Unjust can have place, there must be some coërcive Power, to compell men equally to the performance of the Covenants, by the terrour of some punishment, greater than the benefit they expect by the breach of their Covenant; and to make good that Propriety, which by mutuall Contract men acquire, in recompence of the universall Right they abandon: such power there is none before the erection of a Common-wealth.[43]

These concerns lead Hobbes to an obvious question: Given the state of war and competition, the various human wills each striving after its own good, how can a commonwealth be established?

> The only way to erect such a Common Power, as may be able to defend them from the invasion of Forraigners, and the injuries of one another, and thereby to secure them in such sort, as that by their owne industrie, and by the fruites of the Earth, they may nourish themselves and live contentedly; is, to conferre all their power and strength upon one Man, or upon one Assembly of men, that may reduce all their Wills, by a plurality of voices, unto one Will: which is as much as to say, to appoint one Man, or Assembly of men, to beare their Person; and every one to owne, and acknowledge himselfe to be Author of whatsoever he that so beareth their Person, shall Act, or cause to be Acted, in those thing which concerne the Common Peace and Safetie and therein to submit their Wills, every one to his Will, and their Judgements, to his Judgment. This is more than Consent, or Concord; it is a reall Unitie of them all, in one and the same Person, made by Covenant of every man with every man, in such manner, as if every man should say to every man, *I Authorise and give up my Right of Governing my selfe, to this Man, or to this Assembly of men, on this condition, that thou give up thy Right to him, and Authorise all his Actions in like manner.* This done, the Multitude so united in one Person, is called a COMMON-WEALTH, in latine CIVITAS. This is the Generation of that great LEVIATHAN, or rather (to speake

more reverently) of that *Mortall God*, to which wee owe under the *Immortall God*, our peace and defence.[44]

The Leviathan is formed out of the mutual transference of the right to self-governance to another body, either person or assembly. This is one difficulty in interpreting Hobbes. A singular, strong monarch is not necessary for the Leviathan; thus, the automatic connection of Hobbes with a royalist position is slightly undermined (though the language of a mortal god certainly returns to the divine right of kings rhetoric). Clearly, a singular will (the monarch) is more effective than a plurality of wills attempting to operate as a single will (the Assembly), but theoretically, a well-unified Assembly would be just as much of a Leviathan as any monarch. The purpose of the Leviathan is to defend the commonwealth against threats, both external (foreigners) and internal (injuries of one another). Human nature does not change due to the rule of the Leviathan; we are still concerned with our own safety and well-being. We have created the Leviathan out of that concern, and what keeps humans in check is the coercive threat the Leviathan poses to its own people. This is the coercive power, the threat of terror, that makes breaching the covenant costlier than staying in it (see chapter 3).

## LOCKE

The next major figure in "contract" theory of political philosophy is John Locke. Born when Hobbes was already in his forties, Locke lived through the execution of Charles I, the Commonwealth period, the Protectorate of Cromwell, the restoration under James II, and the Glorious Revolution. Yet Locke was a child during the worst of these events and came into his own as a political thinker after things had calmed considerably. The contextual differences between Hobbes and Locke can be traced to their differing perspectives on the civil wars (consider the respectively similar life experiences of Plato and Aristotle).

Locke's political philosophy, like Hobbes's, is a state of nature and social contract theory. The similarities end there. Locke begins with a discussion of the state of nature:

> To understand political power right, and derive it from its original, we must consider what state all men are naturally in, and that is, a state of perfect freedom to order their actions and dispose of their possessions and persons, as they think fit, within the bounds of the law of nature; without asking leave, or depending upon the will of any other man.[45]

This is a negative conception of liberty, the absence of external constraints, as is Hobbes's. The widest difference between the two is the law of nature within the state of nature. Locke states:

> But though this be a state of liberty, yet it is not a state of licence: though man in that state have an uncontrollable liberty to dispose of his person or possessions, yet he has not liberty to destroy himself, or so much as any creature in his possession, but where some nobler use than its bare preservation calls for it. The state of nature has a law of nature to govern it, which obliges every one: and reason, which is that law, teaches all man-kind, who will but consult it, that being all equal and independent, no one ought to harm another in his life, health, liberty, or possessions: for men being all the workmanship of one omnipotent and infinitely wise Maker; all the servants of one sovereign Master, sent into the world by his order, and about his business; they are his property, whose workmanship they are, made to last during his, not another's pleasure: and being furnished with like faculties, sharing all in one community of nature, there cannot be supposed any such subordination among us that may authorize us to destroy another, as if we were made for one another's uses, as the inferior ranks of creatures are for ours.[46]

Locke's natural law is much more complex than Hobbes's self-preservation model. The Lockean model suggests that God, at least as Creator, can be known through reason.

Locke attempts to deal with the apparent ahistorical aspect of the state of nature.

> It is often asked, as a mighty objection, "where are or ever were there any men in such a state of nature?" To which it may suffice as an answer at present, that since all princes and rulers of independent governments, all through the world, are in a state of nature, it is plain the world never was, nor ever will be, without numbers of men in that state. I have named all governors of independent communities, whether they are, or are not, in league with others: for it is not every compact that puts an end to the state of nature between men, but only this one of agreeing together mutually to enter into one community, and make one body politic; other promises and compacts men may make one with another, and yet still be in the state of nature.[47]

For Locke, humans exist in a state of nature when they are not in their own political system, aliens,[48] those who cannot give consent,[49] and so on. Thus, "princes and rulers" exist in a state of nature toward one another the same way two men on a deserted island exist in relation to one another, but not in relation to those they govern. There is no political body between independent rulers and no ability to form a social contract (transnational political bodies, such as the United Nations or the European Union seem to undermine Locke's position here). The Hobbesian social contract is made between individuals, with the third-party Leviathan being the guarantor and judge between them. This same system is often read into Locke. However, Simmons deconstructs such an argument:

> [Locke] rightly concentrates his attention on one particular aspect of the agreement (the creation of an authorized judge) in his discussion of the state of nature, for it is this aspect of the agreement that solves the fundamental problems of life in the state of nature. It is, however, still only one aspect of the special agreement that creates a civil society. Without the rest of the agreement, men remain in the state of nature. Thus, any acceptable definition of Locke's state of nature must make reference to (or otherwise capture the significance of) the full agreement that alone creates civil society and removes men from their natural condition. Reference only to a part of that agreement, the creation of a common judge with authority, will not suffice.[50]

Something more is needed than an authorized judge to form a Lockean state. The contract which appoints a third-party arbitrator is not a social contract that forms a commonwealth.[51] Simmons rightly argues that in the Lockean system persons remain in a state of nature until they voluntarily join a legitimate political body.[52] This, it seems, is more problematic from an ahistoric position than other aspects of the state of nature. American citizens do not voluntarily choose to be members of the American political body upon reaching eighteen. If we combine the age of majority requirement, that is the knowing and willful consent to voluntarily join the political body, plus Locke's concern for property (the aspect of his thought he is perhaps best known for), we come upon a problem. Locke states:

> Though the earth, and all inferior creatures, be common to all men, yet every man has a property in his own person: this nobody has any right to but himself. The labour of his body, and the work of his hands, we may say, are properly his. Whatsoever then he removes out of the state that nature hath provided, and left it in, he hath mixed his labour with, and joined to it something that is his own, and thereby makes it his property. It being by him removed from the common state nature hath placed it in, it hath by this labour something annexed to it that excludes the common right of other men.[53]

Locke's view of labor, the mixing of labor with some *thing*, is difficult, but not impossible, to translate into the service-based areas of the economy, such as fast-food workers or summer lifeguards. It is in these areas that American laws allow for pre-eighteen-year-olds to earn an income and begin paying taxes. These individuals are thus subject to the laws of the political body they cannot yet voluntarily join.⁵⁴

Of those who have willingly joined a Lockean political system, they seem to do so for what appear to be Hobbesian reasons:

> The only way whereby any one divests himself of his natural liberty [the state of nature], and puts on the bonds of civil society, is by agreeing with other men to join and unite into a community, for their comfortable, safe, and peaceable living one amongst another, in a secure enjoyment of their properties, and a greater security against any that are not of it. This any number of men may do, because it injures not the freedom of the rest; they are left as they were in the liberty of the state of nature. When any number of men have so consented to make one community or government, they are thereby presently incorporated, and make one body politic, wherein the majority have a right to act and conclude the rest.⁵⁵

Though every person is free in the state of nature, it is not the safest state to be in. The Lockean system does understand the political body to be more secure than the state of nature. This still sounds very Hobbesian. However, Locke's state of nature is almost always modified by the concept of liberty, free from the wills of other persons. Hobbes's state of nature can carry the same notion, that is, that the state of nature is freedom from other wills, but the threat of other wills violating this freedom is pushed to the forefront of Hobbes. In Locke, such a concept falls into the background, if not disappearing entirely. Locke's fullest understanding of the violence possible in the state of nature is still highly optimistic and reason-oriented.

> The state of war is a state of enmity and destruction: and therefore declaring by word or action, not a passionate and hasty, but a sedate, settled design upon another man's life, puts him in a state of war with him against whom he has declared such an intention, and so has exposed his life to the other's power to be taken away by him, or any one that joins with him in his defence, and espouses his quarrel; it being reasonable and just, I should have a right to destroy that which threatens me with destruction: for, by the fundamental law of nature, man being to be preserved as much as possible, when all cannot be preserved, the safety of the innocent is to be preferred: and one may destroy a man who makes war upon him, or has discovered an enmity to his being, for the same reason that he may kill a wolf or a lion; because such men are not under the ties of the common law of reason, have no other rule but that of force and violence, and so may be treated as beasts of prey, those dangerous and noxious creatures, that will be sure to destroy him whenever he falls into their power.⁵⁶

Some interesting insights into Locke's political anthropology can be gained here. Like Hobbes, the natural law allows for self-defense. Unlike Hobbes,

Locke's violators of the law of liberty in the state of nature are irrational, like wild animals that need to be put down for the good of the community. Hobbes's state of nature is amoral. The only law is the law of survival, peacefully if possible, not because it is the moral thing to do, but because it carries the greatest chance of survival. Locke not only seems to have a moral component to his state of nature (other people are God's creations and are in some way sacrosanct) but also a moral component when someone causes me to enter a state of war. Self-defense is reasonable and *just*. The irrationality of the other who precipitates the state of war is just as much a moral category as it is an epistemological category. Locke's move to re-moralize the "state of nature" comes at the cost of increasing the tension between the supposed objective rationality which the European philosophers were seeking and the other forms of thinking which appeared subjective to them: honor, status, and religion, three of the most prevalent reasons for violence in human history. Such elements could not form the basis of rational actions in terms of violence. Locke is therefore indirectly responsible for the increasing rationalization which births bureaucracy and the longer process of desacralization.

## ROUSSEAU

The final figure I wish to consider, before turning to a set of events, is Jean-Jacques Rousseau. Rousseau represents a different approach to the question of humanity as a political creature. Some of this difference stems from his very different position in society—an intelligent outsider who becomes an insider, but who never lost his non-traditional views of the societal elite.[57] Though he did not live to see it, he is considered one of the main intellectual forces behind the French Revolution.

Rousseau's haunting line at the beginning of *The Social Contract* is the orienting concern for this aspect of this study: "Man is born free, and he is everywhere in chains. Men who think themselves the masters of others are indeed greater slaves than they."[58] He goes on to claim, "the social order is a sacred right which serves as a basis for all other rights. And as it is not a natural right, it must be one founded on covenants."[59] At the outset, we are faced with a series of concepts: social order, sacred right, natural right, covenants. Rousseau understands the social order beginning with the concept of the family. It is "the oldest of all societies, and the only natural one."[60] Following the ancient Greek and Roman philosophers, Rousseau says,

> The family may therefore perhaps be seen as the first model of political societies: the head of state bears the image of the father, the people the image of his

children, and all, being born free and equal, surrender their freedom only when they see advantage in doing so.[61]

Clearly, we have some Hobbesian echoes in the concept of advantage, but the prominent role of the family unit seems antithetical to some of Hobbes's other positions.

The movement out of the state of nature is the social contract. Rousseau puts the problem this way:

> How to find a form of association which will defend the person and goods of each member with the collective force of all, and under which each individual, while uniting himself with the others, obeys no one but himself, and remains as free as before.[62]

Rousseau is clearly concerned with maintaining a positive conception of liberty. Hobbes and Locke agreed, to an extent, that some forms of liberty would be curtailed in the political system. Rousseau wants to reject any intrusion into the liberty that each person has. As such, Rousseau is forced to go a slightly different direction in his understanding of the state of nature:

> The essential error of Hobbes, Rousseau thought, was to have read back into the state of nature all the human vices which half-socialization had created, and thus to see culturally-produced depravities as "natural" and Hobbesian absolutism, rather than the creation of a feeling of common good, as the remedy for these depravities. "The error of Hobbes and of the philosophers," Rousseau declared, "is to confound natural man with the men they have before their eyes, and to carry into one system a being who can subsist only in another." (*L'État de Guerre*)[63]

Half-socialization needs unpacking before this passage can be fully parsed. Rousseau contends that the individual is transformed by the institutions that give shape to the polity.

> [Rousseau] thought that modern political life divided man against himself, leaving him, with all his merely private and anti-social interests, half in and half out of political society, enjoying neither the amoral independence of nature nor the moral elevation afforded by true socialization.
>
> The defect of modern politics, in Rousseau's view, was that it was insufficiently political; it compromised between the utter artificiality and communality of political life and the naturalness and independence of pre-political life, and in so doing caused the greatest misfortunes of modern man: self-division, conflict between private will and the common good, a sense of being neither in one condition nor another.[64]

The political human is "anti-natural"[65] and vices arise in the attempt to navigate the political and the natural. This is the phenomenon of half-socialization; of being born free, but everywhere in chains. Rousseau suggests that the Leviathan of Hobbes only deals with the surface symptoms of political life. In a way, it absorbs the "conflict between private will and the common good" through the threat of punishment if the private will of an individual goes against the common good.[66] Part of the problem lies in the relationship of the state to the dominant religious faction. This is the par excellence example in Rousseau of self-division. After praising a sort of Protestant pietism ("without temples, altars or rituals, and limited to inward devotion to the supreme God") which he calls "the religion of man" and differentiating it from "the religion of the citizen" which is the "religion established in a single country" which carries the force of law behind it, Rousseau moves on to his true target.[67]

> There is a third and more curious kind of religion, which, giving men two legislative orders, two rulers, two homelands, puts them under two contradictory obligations, and prevents their being at the same time both churchmen and citizens. Such is the religion of the Lamas, the Japanese, and such is Catholic Christianity.[68]

Rousseau has criticisms of all three of these possibilities. Christians under the Gospel would be terrible citizens because this type of Christianity is too focused on the spiritual. The citizens' religion leads to intolerance and holy wars. The third option, which he saw particularly in France, Rousseau dismisses out of hand, on the grounds that, "Everything that destroys social unity is worthless; and all institutions that set man at odds with himself are worthless."[69] Rousseau famously suggests that a secularized, tolerant version of the religion of the citizen is the best way to bind the political community together in unity. Rousseau explains this notion of a civil religion as follows:

> The dogmas of the civil religion must be simple and few in number, expressed precisely and without explanations or commentaries. The existence of an omnipotent, intelligent, benevolent deity that foresees and provides; the life to come; the happiness of the just; the punishment of sinners; the sanctity of the social contract and the law—these are the positive dogmas. As for the negative dogmas, I would limit them to a single one: no intolerance. Intolerance is something which belongs to the religions we have rejected.[70]

Rousseau's conception of civil religion helps to underlie his political anthropology. Humans need a single loyalty to focus their will. When loyalties are divided among several institutions, the possibility of internal conflict

## DESACRALIZATION IN PROCESS: THE FRENCH REVOLUTION

Whatever continuity remained between eighteenth-century Europe and its medieval past was severed with the execution of Louis XVI.[71] For all the emphasis placed on the American War of Independence, it is, in fact, the French Revolution which sets the course for nineteenth- and twentieth-century political philosophy. William H. Sewell Jr. suggests three criteria for "a historical event . . . (1) a ramified sequence of occurrences that (2) is recognized as notable by contemporaries, and that (3) results in a durable transformation of structures."[72] The American War of Independence was not "revolutionary" in the same sense as its French counterpart. Structurally, the only major changes were of the executive branch (removing the king and separating the prime minister from the House of Commons) and the lack of a single state Church. But these are not the ground-shaking types of changes that move from "event" to "revolution." British society lived on in the former colonies, especially the Common Law system.

The foregoing is not to demean the historical importance of the American War of Independence. However, it serves as a foil for the actual revolution at the end of the eighteenth century. The French Revolution was properly a revolution, a turning about of society, culture, law, politics, and religion. It is one thing to accuse the king of being a tyrant; it is another to remove his head. Yet the interpretation of the French Revolution is still hotly debated. On the political right,[73] the Revolution is seen as an example of the dangers of a wholesale rejection of the institutions and traditions which had held a population together. This view stems from Edmund Burke's *Reflections on the Revolution in France* and contemporaneous conservative French thinkers (de Bonald, Maistre). On the political left, the Revolution is seen as one of the first proletarian uprisings of the modern period which succeeded in giving power to the lower classes, followed by the conservative reaction of Bonaparte and the brief restoration of the monarchy, followed by another uprising of the people. This view becomes prominent in the 1960s (a time of more uprisings) as Marxist theorists moved away from the actions of Marxist regimes. A third possibility stems from de Tocqueville; the Revolution merely solidified an empyreal revolution that was already underway.

Modernity had already come to the French through State centralization; the Revolution simply accelerated the move toward the fully modern mindset. We need not determine which side of the debate is correct, other than to say that all are. The French Revolution does represent a proletarian rejection of the elite and an attempt to level society, lines which the founders of the United States of America were unwilling to cross to the same degree. Likewise, "the Terror" represents the breakdown in society caused by the vacuum of the power symbol of the throne and the anti-clericalism that accompanied it. But such options are only available in a modernizing society which is well along in the centralizing process.[74]

The germane aspects of the French Revolution center on the people as sovereign. The Revolutionary leaders faced a two-pronged but singular problem: articulating "the will of the people" and *representing* sovereignty."[75] The two are interconnected due to the newness of the problem. Unlike the British Parliament, which had undergone the pains of civil wars (see above), the French Estates-General had not met for more than a century until the financial crises of the late eighteenth century forced the monarchy to reconvene the body. The National Assembly, formed through the will of the people, quickly faced problems of international law (as it existed in the eighteenth century) for Corsica, Alsace, and Avignon. While the particulars need not trouble us here, the resulting incidents required the National Assembly to violate/rework the meaning of various treaties which the French monarchy had entered over the previous centuries.[76] Thus, the National Assembly put itself above the previous legal system and operated out of a state of exception.

However, they also attempted to curtail certain aspects of popular sovereignty within the established borders of France. If the popular will of Corsica could be invoked to join France, could the popular will of Breton be invoked to leave France?[77] Members of the National Assembly used quasi-ethnic arguments for the unity and indivisibility of some areas. Brittany could not become a separate state due to the French-ness of its populace, whereas Corsica was not really Genoese, and the Alsatians were not really German. The majority of France could vote to allow Brittany to break away in an expression of the entire popular will, not merely the Bretons' own will.[78]

Ernst Kantorowicz explains the representation of royal sovereignty in the metaphor of the "King's Two Bodies" but the diffusion of the populace (see below for comments on diffusion) creates a situation in which someone (or a group) must claim to speak on behalf of the people as a channel for the "will of the people" to be executed in the political sphere. The king has two bodies, the natural (e.g., Richard III, Henry VIII, or Victoria), which is born, grows old, and dies. The other body is the immortal body of *The King* or the political body. This body never dies because it is the concentration of royal power in the symbol of the throne. As political theology, this is the body of Christ as Jesus of Nazareth and the body of Christ as the Eucharist/Church.[79] When politicians (especially in the American context) claim that "the people" want some type of legislation passed or action to be performed it is a rhetorical nod to the symbol of power in a democracy in order to strengthen the position of that legislation. The symbol of the presidency is more often a point of contention between various political factions than a symbol of unity, hence the need by politicians to transcend contested symbols by turning to abstract symbols that are filled with meaning by the listener. Consider the example of tax legislation and the phrase "the American people want lower taxes." Someone who also wants lower taxes will identify with "the American people" but opponents of lower taxes do not hear "American people"; instead, they hear "upper-class" and believe that the politician is ignoring the will of the *real* American people. The symbol of "the People" is much like Teflon, nothing sticks to it as everyone can redefine it to their own in-group. But the singular offices, such as president, senate majority leader, and speaker of the house, cannot be pure symbols because real people, not a metaphorical conglomeration, occupy those offices. However, declarations of war or fundamental shifts in society made on behalf of "the people" are couched in "exceptional" language. To put it another way, "crisis" is not used as in the previous example of tax legislation in the same manner as the War on Terror, the environmental crisis (where it appears in the actual language), or the health care system. A state of exception, a la Schmitt, can only be declared by the sovereign. What we see in the shift from royal to popular sovereignty is the change in who can make the declaration: experts, or in Reed's terminology, those represented as experts.

## FROM THEORY TO TYPES

I now turn to the construction of a typology of sovereignty which exists in two separate binary categories. The first binary, centralized/diffuse, refers to the locus of sovereignty. "Centralized" sovereignty means that sovereignty is held by no more than a dozen persons, all of whom tend to act (at least publicly) with a single will. The sovereign could, in this system, be a single ruler or a committee with a small number of members who, for various reasons, present a unified front to the outside world. "Diffuse" sovereignty means that sovereignty is held by a larger group,[80] be it a larger committee, multiple committees, or individuals of a particular type. The sovereign is non-existent, but sovereignty is still applicable to those in certain roles or with certain characteristics. The second binary, actual/metaphorical, refers to the power inherent in the locus of sovereignty. "Actual" in this case means the realistic probability that the dictates of the sovereign will come to pass.[81] The monarch who renders the death sentence on an individual, and then proceeds to kill that individual personally, has fully actualized sovereign power. Of course, little in the way of sovereignty is conducted on a one-to-one basis. It is more likely that the monarch will call upon an executioner to carry out the execution. No matter how trustworthy the guards or the executioner, a note of possibility has entered that the prisoner will not be executed even though the monarch has commanded it. The individual may escape or be rescued, thwarting the monarch's wishes and by extension, sovereignty. It should be noted that external pressures on the monarch, such as a religious figure interceding for the prisoner or the masses pleading (or demanding) his release, would not be a nullification of the monarch's sovereignty. If the monarch changes course, that is part of sovereign power, even if the original impetus comes from an external source. "Metaphorical" refers to the lack of likelihood that the will of the sovereign will come to pass. King John can pronounce the death sentence on Robin Hood all he likes, but while Robin Hood is safe in Sherwood Forest with mass popularity among the peasants, it is unlikely that John's will can be actualized.

The double-axis typology is a reworking, or inversion, of Weber's theory of *Herrschaft*, legitimate authority. I contend that an objective standpoint—how someone outside the authority system understands the relationship structure between the authority figure and the subject—is a better way to conceptualize sovereignty as opposed to authority. Authority is bestowed through the complex interaction of cultural norms in addition to the subjective standpoint.[82] The cultural norms help to balance the power differences between the authority figure and the subject. Sovereignty is an objective asymmetrical power relationship, which can still take the subjective element as a part of the system. Metaphorical sovereignty, that is, the inability of the sovereign to enforce its will, is a way of objectively understanding or measuring the subjective viewpoint. The subject may believe and act as if the authority does have authoritative power, while the observer notes that such beliefs are unwarranted and actions misguided.

The previous discussion calls for an answer to the question "What is power?" At its base, power is physical, a matter of life and death. Advances in technology to do physical harm have always been at the forefront of human history. From the knife to the bow to the musket to the atomic bomb, humans are quite adept at making things that kill other things. While this type of power is certainly the most important in terms of consequences, it is not the only form of power that operates. Political power is closely connected with *authorized* physical power. As Weber notes:

34                                Chapter 1

The state is the human community that, within a defined territory—and the key word here is "territory"—(successfully) claims the *monopoly of legitimate force* for itself. The specific characteristic of the present is that the right to use physical force is only granted to any other associations or individuals to the extent that the *state* itself permits this. The state is seen as the sole source of the "right" to use force.[83]

Politics, then, "means the attempt to gain a share of power or to influence the distribution of power, whether it be among states or among groups of people living within a state."[84] The political community functions similarly:

> The term "political community" shall apply to a community whose social action is aimed at subordinating to orderly domination by the participants a "territory" and the conduct of the persons within it, through readiness to resort to physical force, including normally force of arms.[85]

This suggests that political power resides in those who are involved in the decision-making process concerning who gets to use physical force.[86] The famous statement of von Clausewitz should be inverted: "Politics is war by other means." This would fit with a Hobbesian view of human existence: "A war of all upon all," is only checked by the power of the Leviathan.

Weber acknowledges the "authoritarian" possibility of other types of power.[87] The financial and cultural power of the Prussian state to early Germany and New York City to the United States gives each a certain amount of power over their respective nations. Yet it is not clear that these examples of non-physical power meet the definition of sovereignty offered up by Schmitt. To put it another way: Is there such a thing as an economic "exception" which would require the type of sovereignty formulated by Schmitt? The immediate aftermath of the 2008 financial crisis suggests that there is such a sovereign, or at the least, an association of institutions that act as a sovereign (see chapter 4). Cultural "sovereignty" is either an illusion or the most contested form of sovereignty one can imagine. The "production" of culture has historically been tied to a region: eighteenth-century Paris, nineteenth-century New York, twentieth-century Hollywood, and so on. But to understand sovereignty in such terms would require the "exception" before even dealing with the multiple sites of cultural production in the globalized world and the deeper problem of cultural as taste.[88] The best expression of cultural "sovereignty" occurs in a phenomenon such as the #MeToo movement where a transnational cultural zeitgeist has the power to banish formerly powerful individuals. This zeitgeist creates the exception by ruling the court of public opinion in which the judicial rules of due process are replaced by sudden outrage. Individuals (or institutions) channel the zeitgeist at perceived perpetrators, allowing the exception to last until the power of the zeitgeist is broken or runs out of cultural capital.[89]

My contention is not that Weber is wrong in his theory of dominion, but that to generate a theory of sovereignty requires more than Weber gives in his theory of domination. Not all of Weber's categories of domination can be translated into theories of sovereignty; as noted above, some may be dead ends for a concept of sovereignty (culture), while others are notoriously difficult to track (economics). Each of these spheres represents sites of sovereign conflicts and the multiple avenues in which these conflicts are negotiated. Bourdieu hints at these spheres, but due to a different set of concerns, he also does not investigate the problem of sovereignty.[90]

My sketch of sovereignty is currently missing one key component, which has been implied in a number of ways but requires another step in the hermeneutical spiral to put it in conversation with sovereignty as a concept. In the next chapter, I turn to the nature of bureaucratic systems, but we must "look ahead" to clarify some aspects of sovereignty.

Bureaucratic systems help to moderate the double-axis typology of sovereignty. Centralized power systems are expanded through the bureaucratic structures, while diffuse power systems are solidified through the use of a single bureaucratic regime. Likewise, actual sovereignty is diluted through the levels of bureaucracy, while metaphorical sovereignty at least takes visible and structural form. The bureaucratic system does not fundamentally alter the underlying power elements; for example, a diffuse sovereignty will still be diffuse, but less diffuse than without the bureaucracy. I will expand on these points in the next chapter.

## NOTES

1. Any number of works exist on Weber, both on his life and his thought. Of particular note is Arthur Mitzman, *The Iron Cage: An Historical Interpretation of Max Weber* (New York: Alfred A. Knopf, 1970), which employs psychoanalysis to relate Weber's life to his work, and Lawrence A. Scaff, *Fleeing the Iron Cage: Culture, Politics, and Modernity in the Thought of Max Weber* (Berkley, CA: University of California Press, 1989), which is a historically contextualized approach to the same.

2. Max Weber, *Economy and Society: An Outline of Interpretive Sociology*, ed. Guenther Roth and Claus Wittich, 2 vols. (New York: Bedminster Press, 1968), 954. Hereinafter *ES*. Note that Weber's use of "tradition" is socio-historical, while MacIntyre uses "tradition" in a historical-philosophical way.

3. Max Weber, "Politics as a Vocation," in *Max Weber's Complete Writings on Academic and Political Vocations*, ed. John Dreijmanis, trans. Gordon C. Wells (New York: Algora Publishing, 2008). Hereinafter *PV*.

4. Ibid.

5. Hannah Arendt, *The Origins of Totalitarianism* (New York: Houghton Mifflin Harcourt Publishing Co., 1948), 339, n.65. Emphasis added.

6. Thanks goes to the Political Theology Network online discussion of Schmitt's *Political Theology*, Fall 2018, for this insight.

7. Schmitt, 5.

8. On religion and the French Revolution, see Michael Burleigh, *Earthly Powers: The Clash of Religion and Politics from the French Revolution to the Great War* (New York: HarperCollins, 2005).

9. Michael Hollerich, "Carl Schmitt," in Scott and Cavanaugh, 112.

10. References to both Mommsen and Habermas appear in Pedro T. Magalhães, "A Contingent Affinity: Max Weber, Carl Schmitt, and the Challenge of Modern Politics," *Journal of the History of Ideas* 77, no. 2 (April 2016): 283–304. Magalhães ultimately rejects Habermas's claims, 304.

11. See my comments on Rousseau's "civil religion" below.

12. The nearly 800-member body House of Lords is not chosen on a representative basis, which complicates the application of this discussion to the UK.

13. "2016 Michigan Results," *New York Times*, August 1, 2017, https://www.nytimes.com/elections/2016/results/michigan.

14. Patricia Mazzei, Frances Robles, and Maggie Astor, "Rick Scott Wins Florida Senate Recount as Bill Nelson Concedes," *The New York Times*, November 28, 2018, sec. U.S., https://www.nytimes.com/2018/11/18/us/florida-recount-senate-rick-scott-bill-nelson.html (Accessed December 30, 2018).

15. The most at any onetime in Anglo-American history seems to have been the mid-2010s in the lead-up to the Brexit vote, with the Tories, Labour, Liberal-Democrats, and the UK Independence Party (UKIP) each playing a role. Canadian and Australian governments are usually lead, either alone of as the major block of a coalition, by one of the two major parties in their respective systems.

16. See the Introduction to Ronald M. Glassman, William H. Swatos Jr., and Paul L. Rosen, eds., *Bureaucracy Against Democracy and Socialism* (New York: Greenwood Press, 1987), where Weber is compared to the "weeping prophet," Jeremiah.

17. Giorgio Agamben, *The Kingdom and the Glory: For a Theological Genealogy of Economy and Government*, trans. Lorenzo Chiesa and Matteo Mandarini (Stanford, CA: Stanford University Press, 2011), 3–4.

18. There is a related question—is the tension in modernity with "religion" or particularly Christian (of the "orthodox" or "conservative" type) claims? I lean toward the latter.

19. This is, by necessity, a broad statement in which the exceptions prove the rule. The only serious outlier is England due to its alternate form of reformation.

20. Robert Nisbet, *The Quest for Community: A Study in the Ethics of Order and Freedom* (Willington, DE: ISI Books, 2010), 113–120.

21. Ibid., 121.

22. Ellen Meiksins Wood, *Liberty and Property: A Social History of Western Political Thought from Renaissance to Enlightenment* (New York: Verso, 2012), 224.

23. Ibid.

24. George Yerby, *People and Parliament: Representative Rights and the English Revolution* (New York: Palgrave MacMillan, 2008), 145.

25. George H. Sabine, *A History of Political Theory* (New York: Henry Holt and Company, 1937), 456, n1.

26. Ibid., 456.

27. Ibid., 458.

28. Ibid.

29. Thomas Hobbes, *Leviathan*, ed. G. A. J. Rogers and Karl Schuhmann (London: Thoemmes Continuum, 2005), 9. I have retained the Old English spellings and forms of emphasis.

30. Ibid., 99.

31. Ibid., 100.

32. Ibid., 101.

33. Ibid., 102.

34. Ibid., 103.

35. Ibid., 104.

36. Ibid.

37. Ibid.

38. Ibid., 105, emphasis in original.

39. Ibid., 106.

40. Ibid., 107.

41. Ibid., 107 and 111.

42. Ibid., 115.

43. Ibid.

44. Ibid., 136–137.

45. John Locke, *Two Treatises of Government: And a Letter Concerning Toleration*, ed. Ian Shapiro (New Haven, CT: Yale University Press, 2003), Second Treatise, II, §4. All references will be to the Second Treatise, with the Roman numerals indicating chapter and Arabic numerals the section.

46. Ibid., II, §6.

47. Ibid., II, §14.

48. Ibid., II, §9.

49. Ibid., II, §15.

50. A. John Simmons, "Locke's State of Nature," in *The Social Contract Theorists: Critical Essays on Hobbes, Locke, and Rousseau*, ed. Christopher W. Morris, Critical Essays on the Classics (Lanham, MD: Rowman & Littlefield Publishers, 1999), 102.

51. Ibid., 101.

52. Ibid., 103, where Simmons uses a negative form to make the point.

53. Locke, II, §26.

54. This is not to say that only tax-paying minors are under the laws of the political body, or we would have no need for juvenile detention centers. For Locke's comments on children (which I do not believe solve the problem of pre-majority participation in American political life), see Locke, VI, §58–94.

55. Locke, VIII, §95.

56. Locke, III, §16.

57. Helena Rosenblatt, *Rousseau and Geneva: From the First Discourse to The Social Contract, 1749–1762*, Ideas in Context (Cambridge: Cambridge University Press, 1997), 29–41.

58. Jean-Jacques Rousseau, *The Social Contract*, trans. Maurice Cranston (New York: Penguin Books, 2006), I.1. Roman numerals will indicate the book number, while Arabic numerals will indicate the chapter.

59. Ibid.

60. Ibid., I.2.

61. Ibid.

62. Ibid., I.6.

63. Patrick Riley, "A Possible Explanation of Rousseau's General Will," in Morris, 172.

64. Ibid., 169.

65. Ibid.

66. One would hope that punishments would only result after the actualization (or planned actualization, in the case of conspiracy to commit a crime). The Leviathan is too often linked with authoritarian despots and not often enough to coercive power per se.

67. Rousseau, IV.8.

68. Ibid.

69. Ibid.

70. Ibid., IV.8. It must be noted that the words Rousseau uses to describe the deity require a multitude of explanations and commentaries, to say nothing of the life to come. Rousseau's civil religion does not solve the problem of interpretation. Could Rousseau's civil religion "tolerate" a rejection of "the life to come"?

71. Pun very much intended.

72. For Sewell, a historical event is the type of moment(s) in history with which historians concern themselves. Everything in the past is a historical event, but only some things are *Events*; William H. Sewell Jr., *The Logics of History: Social Theory and Social Transformation* (Chicago, IL: University of Chicago Press, 2005), 228.

73. It is fitting to use the otherwise problematic "right" and "left" in the context of the French Revolution, as it was the Jacobins who sat on the left-hand side of the French Assembly while the conservatives sat on the right. This seating arrangement has been the metaphor for shorthand political labeling ever since.

74. See the brief discussion on de Tocqueville in Isaac Ariail Reed, "Power and the French Revolution: Toward a Sociology of Sovereignty," *Historicka Sociologie*, no. 1 (2018): 47–70 (here, 48–50), https://doi.org/10.14712/23363525.2018.38.

75. Ibid., 55 (emphasis original).

76. Edward James Kolla, *Sovereignty, International Law, and the French Revolution* (New York: Cambridge University Press, 2017), 35–83.

77. Ibid., 80, where Kolla notes the similar discourse used to justify Southern secession before the American Civil War.

78. This paragraph draws from Kolla, 74–80.

79. The split between the Eucharistic body and the Ecclesial body of the twelfth century is interesting, but not critical to this study. See António Bento, "From the Medieval Church as a Mystical Body to the Modern State as a Mystical Person: Ernst Kantorowicz and Carl Schmitt," in *Political Theology in Medieval and Early Modern Europe: Discourses, Rites, and Representations*, ed. Montserrat Herrero, Jaume Aurell, and Angela C. Miceli Stout (Turnhout, Belgium: Brepols, 2017), 65–85.

80. Weber, *ES*, 952.

81. My use of "actual" should not be confused with Agamben's discussion of potentiality/actualization of sovereignty in his *Homo Sacer*. See Giorgio Agamben, *Homo Sacer: Sovereign Power and Bare Life* (Stanford, CA: Stanford University Press, 1998), 37–48.

82. On the problems of the concept of "authority" in political theology, see O'Donovan, 16–17.

83. Weber, *PV*, 156. Emphasis original. Needless to say, modern military doctrines of power projection and the economic realities of globalization call into question Weber's (and by extension, Bourdieu's) emphasis on territory, both in militaristic and other forms of domination.

84. Ibid.

85. Weber, *ES*, 901.

86. Or "symbolic violence"; see Pierre Bourdieu, "Rethinking the State: The Genesis and Structure of the Bureaucratic Field," trans. Loïc J. D. Wacquant and Samar Farage, *Sociological Theory* 12, no. 1 (March 1994): 3.

87. Weber, *ES*, 946.

88. For instance, India's "Bollywood" film industry produces more films than Hollywood; however, the numbers do not displace the global understanding of Hollywood. Viral videos, memes, and posts reflect a democratization of cultural production, but these means are only accessible through certain gatekeepers (Facebook, Twitter, YouTube, etc.). Cultural production still requires patronage, but patronage is not sovereignty.

89. I return to the #MeToo Movement in chapter 2 and approach the issue from a different angle. However, in the context of zeitgeist/mistake, consider the situation of comedian and actor Aziz Ansari. There is also the problem of such zeitgeist attempting to migrate from cultural condemnation to judicial condemnation. In this case, the differing rules (due process, the inability to adjudicate "he said/she said" arguments, and the need for evidence) can begin to undo the prevailing *zeitgeist*. On Ansari, see Bari Weiss, "Guilty of Not Being a Mind Reader," *The New York Times*, January 17, 2018.

90. Bourdieu, "Rethinking," 1–6.

# 2

## Who Coerces the Coercers?

In this chapter, I argue that coercion is ultimately a tactic, a means to some other end. Yet coercion (or coercion as the basis of political power) is so prevalent that it has become invisible. Here, I explain how coercion functions on a theoretical level in both philosophy and law. I then describe the way in which coercion has become a ubiquitous part of Western society as an expression of sovereign power.[1]

### COERCION AS PHILOSOPHY AND LAW

While sovereignty is a concept in the theo-political realm, coercion is used in both philosophy and legal aspects, with a list of synonyms such as "duress" and "threat" complicating the semantic landscape. One of the most important studies on coercion, Alan Wertheimer's *Coercion*, operates on this philosophical/legal distinction but also provides some important qualifiers as to how far the distinction can go:

> For better or worse, our moral views about coercion are somewhat inchoate. The law, by its very nature, attempts to make those inchoate beliefs reasonably consistent and explicit. True, judges discuss coercion "in the law," whereas philosophers are concerned with "morality." It would, however, be wrong to make too much of this. The law's interest in coercion reflects our moral views about the conditions under which persons should be held responsible for their acts. And thus the law gives us a lens through which we can see and analyze these moral notions at work.[2]

In both law and philosophy, coercion is understood as the absence of freedom.[3] This distinction goes back at least to Aristotle, where he distinguishes between voluntary, involuntary, and non-voluntary actions:

Such actions are mixed, although they seem more like voluntary than involuntary ones; because at the time that they are performed they are matters of choice, and the end of the action varies with the occasion; so the terms voluntary and involuntary should be used with reference to the time when the actions are performed.[4]

Thus, at the moment the man acts dishonorably to save his family or when the sailors throw their cargo overboard to save their lives (Aristotle's examples), each acts voluntarily insofar as each has control over their actions. This is contrasted with the person in a sailboat driven by the wind where the wind compels the boat, leaving the passenger in an involuntary state. But considered in the abstract, without the specific circumstances, one would not choose to act dishonorably or destroy one's own property.[5] Coercion mixes the voluntary and involuntary aspects.

Modern psychology rightly calls into question the notion of "voluntary" in Aristotelian and Thomistic bio-physiology. Very few, if any, actions are properly undertaken in a "moment." There is a complex set of factors and variables that undergird the action taken by any individual for any reason: genetics, personality, background, mood, even one's state of hunger at the moment of action can affect the outcome.[6] However, the pre-modern philosophers do point to the difficulty for outside observers to determine the "freedom" in another's acts.[7] This is certainly a problem in situations in which the assignment of blame/guilt is a *necessary* component—the judicial system— in contrast to the musings of ethicists in thought experiments. Wertheimer attempts to bridge this gap through an "empirical or a moralized account of the baseline" which functions as a "common-sense" or "reasonable person" standard.[8] In philosophical terminology:

> A *threatens* B by proposing to make B *worse* off relative to some baseline; A makes an *offer* to B by proposing to make B *better* off relative to some baseline. More precisely, A makes a threat when, if B does *not* accept A's proposal, B will be worse off than in the relevant baseline position. A makes an offer when, if B does *not* accept A's proposal, he will be *no* worse off than in the relevant baseline position.[9]

The baseline functions as an assessment of the situation from the "reasonable person," a legal fiction in the Anglo-American common law system that stands for the ordinary person who has had no specialized knowledge of the situation. The reasonable person could also be called the rational person, not that such a person must always be rational, but that the actions of the individual are "justified" under the circumstances.[10] Justification of someone else's actions necessitates an understanding of the empirical evidence, in both a physical and psychological sense, in order to come to a rational decision on whether the act was justified. The language of rationality, a key marker of Weber's bureaucratic mindset (see below), permeates the legal field.

Returning to the distinction between offer and threat, Wertheimer uses two examples:

> *The Stock Market Case.* A realizes that B is about to lose a large sum in the stock market. A tells B that he will help B avoid the loss if and only if B gives him a percent of the amount he would have lost.
>
> *The Ambulance Case.* A comes upon an auto wreck and an injured B on a desolate stretch of the road. A tells B that he will call an ambulance if and only if B gives him $100.[11]

According to Wertheimer, the Stock Market Case is an offer and the Ambulance Case is a threat because, in part, a reasonable person would not make demands of a physically injured and desperate person, while the reasonable person is also familiar (in a broad sense) with the risks associated with the stock market and the role of financial advisors. The reasonable person imagines a degree of detachment from the offer/threat, which ignores, or at the very least underestimates the complex psychological make-up of any individual. It is possible in the Stock Market Case that A is being coercive because of some aspect of B's situation (e.g., chronic medical issues which require large amounts of money). However, there is a sense in which the Stock Market Case is less coercive in that A alerts B to the problem; B could reject A's offer/threat and go to C for the same quality of help.[12] A would be more coercive if she required B to pay before letting B know the details of the impending portfolio problem, as A's behavior in the Ambulance Case is likewise predicated on pre-acceptance of the terms.

While the reasonable person standard is a good starting place, the baseline approach is called into question by Joan McGregor, who rightly points out that the morality of the baseline is left unexamined. Barrera explains:

> For example, people who are destitute can hardly get any worse, and by the normalcy criterion, most proposals they get, no matter how coercive or exploitative, would have to be viewed as offers rather than as intimidating threats because they make the poor better off given the dismal baseline from which they start in their pre-proposal state.[13]

McGregor argues that a baseline approach is only possible in a "perfectly competitive market," which requires:

> 1. There must be enough small (relative to the size of the total market) sellers and buyers of the goods to eliminate the possibility that any single seller or buyer could influence the price of the good. 2. The good produced by each seller must

be identical to that made by every other seller, which is the same as saying that the goods are homogeneous. 3. Firms, as well as all resources and inputs, must be mobile in the sense that there are no barriers or impediments preventing them from entering or leaving the industry (costless entry and exit, no externalities or transaction costs). 4. There must be perfect knowledge, meaning that all participants in the economic process must know all costs and prices in which they have an economic interest, and they must know the outcome of all economic events pertaining to them.[14]

Such a system is closer to a philosophical thought experiment than a Weberian ideal-type. That is, such a market cannot exist because of scarcity, beyond the problem of "perfect knowledge." However, instead of this undermining her, it in fact proves McGregor's point; the playing field is not even for all parties, and starting from the position of a "neutral" baseline is problematic, if not completely nonsensical.

Given McGregor's concerns, I will posit a unique definition of coercion as the *activation*, or *threat of activation*, of some *negative consequence*, in an attempt to *persuade* another to act (that is, do/think) as the coercer *desires*.[15] A coerces B when A threatens or carries out a threat on B's interests unless B acts in the way A has commanded. I will unpack these elements in turn. First, "activation" or threat thereof points to the possibility of direct or indirect action by the coercer. In the Ambulance Case, A's non-action is the threat, given that the reasonable person standard would require A to act to help B.[16] In the Stock Market Case, A is under no moral or legal obligation to act.[17] A acting on B's behalf is an offer; A's non-action does not rise to the level of coercion. This is directly related to *negative consequences*. All situations where the negative consequence stems directly from an activation, not from a non-action, are necessarily coercive. Non-actions must be judged on a case-by-case basis. "Persuasion" returns to the Aristotelian "mixed" action. The action the coercer desires the coerced to take is (generally) one the coercer cannot undertake.[18] The coercer inverts the cost-benefit analysis of performing the act. Where usually undertaking the action in question produces more negative consequences than non-action for the coerced, the coercer makes non-action the source of greater negative consequences. Finally, the coercer (usually) has some self-interest in the action to be undertaken. The coercer desires a certain state of affairs and uses another to achieve it.[19] Coercion cannot exist where an individual already desires to do the action; I cannot coerce my children into eating candy when they are asking for that very candy. I can, however, use the candy as part of coercing them to eat broccoli, so long as candy is not portrayed as an award for eating the broccoli. Though the two phrases "If you don't eat your broccoli, you won't get candy," and "If you eat your broccoli, you'll get candy" are conceptually similar, the first is coercive while the second is an offer because candy is presumed in the first situation, while it is not presumed in the second. Both coercion and offers are regularly used in the education of young children. If a class always has outdoor recess but the students are inattentive to the teacher, she may coerce their good behavior by threatening the removal of recess. She could, on the other hand, encourage them to pay attention by offering to extend their recess time. I believe this definition and examples adequately deal with the problems McGregor raises by avoiding "baseline" terminology and turning to "negative" outcomes based on the reasonable person criterion from the position of the coerced. My definition also avoids the problems of focusing too greatly on the concept of violence.[20]

However, returning to Wertheimer's concern for legal examples, it must be noted that the threat of negative consequences does not rise to the level of coercion if the victim has a reasonable alternative.

> A threat, even if improper, does not amount to duress if the victim has a reasonable alternative to succumbing and fails to take advantage of it. It is sometimes said that the threat must arouse such fear as precludes a party from exercising free will and judgment or that it must be such as would induce assent on the part of a brave man or a man of ordinary firmness. The rule stated in this Section omits any such requirement because of its vagueness and impracticability. It is enough if the threat actually induces assent . . . on the part of one who has no reasonable alternative.[21]

This theory holds in both legal and philosophical settings as well. On the legal side, coercion is a criminal act insofar as it deals with the threat of violence or other legally protected areas.

> In the paradigm case of *extortion*, A receives property or some other benefit from B by proposing to commit a violent crime against B; extortion is, therefore, assimilable to the crime of robbery. And while it might, at first glance, be thought that the extortive threat itself is mere *speech*, that it should not be punished if unaccompanied by any other wrongful act or transaction, the criminalization of extortive threats can, without great difficulty, be assimilated to the (uncontroversial) criminalization of *attempted* robbery or assault.[22]

Here, coercion is the proposal of violence, the basis of various crimes from simple mugging to more complex situations such as armed robbery. Blackmail, on the other hand, is more complex.

> The criminalization of speech is more problematic if A *blackmails* B, as when A threatens to reveal damaging or embarrassing information. For unlike the typical case of extortion, where A threatens to commit an act that is

independently illegal, a blackmailer may threaten to commit an act that is, in itself, legally permissible. A may have a right to reveal information about B, A may have a right to sell the information to someone else who may reveal it, and A may have a right to sell the information directly to B. Yet A blackmails B if A *threatens* to publicize or transfer the information *unless* B buys the information from him.[23]

The individual elements of blackmail may be entirely legal. Given no other wrongdoing,[24] if I happen upon a neighbor engaged in an affair, there is nothing that legally prevents me from informing the respective partners; in fact, I may have a certain (moral) obligation to do so. There is also nothing that legally prevents me from informing others or selling the story to a tabloid, though here the morality of the situation changes in that I may have a moral obligation to not spread gossip, even if true.[25] However, if I threaten the adulterer with the revelation of the affair unless I am paid, I have committed blackmail.

The quintessential example of coercion is sexual harassment. The #MeToo movement has brought extra attention to both use-of-force (sexual assault) and non-force (sexual harassment)[26] coercive aspects of sexual harassment. This has been especially the case in Hollywood and statehouses (including Washington, DC), where the power imbalance between established male producers/politicians and up-and-coming female actresses/interns is clear.[27] However, does the power disparity indicate per se coercion and thus harassment? Or does the power imbalance merely increase the odds of coercion, but not necessarily imply it? A formal offer (good for $x$, good for $y$) is clearly distinguished from formal coercion (good for $x$, bad for $y$). Offers can also take the form of good and bad for both parties (good and bad for $x$, good and bad for $y$) as in the case of any honest negotiation or compromise. What of good for one party and good and bad for the other (good for $x$, good and bad for $y$)? Is this coercion, or an imbalanced offer? Does the degree of separation between the good and the bad play into the coercion/offer debate? To put it another way, is there a threshold at which offer becomes coercion? Does the negative have to outweigh the positive? These questions highlight the difficulty of the offer/coercion problem (especially in the #MeToo context).

Philosophy has another way of dealing with coercion vis-à-vis metaphysical conceptions of *freedom*. Can one be considered free while acting under the coercion of another? Metaphysical freedom is understood as the ability to choose $x$ or *not x* whenever $x$ is a possible option. Thus, I maintain my metaphysical freedom even when I cannot choose between flying like Superman and not flying, because flying like Superman is not a true possibility for me. We could remove the moral aspect of coercion and apply it to some abstraction, gravity for instance. I could then claim that I am coerced by gravity to of ordering becomes the reason given. There is no reason given for why one should follow the orders of the authority. To put it another way, Morris's "authority" seems to be sui generis; it has no history of development. It may be that rational reason-giving (whether Weberian or Rawlsian) is better than the raw application of power as the reason, but Morris's framework seems to lack this distinction.

Thus, we see the superiority of Weber's sociological politics. Violence is the beginning of any political system; it is "absolutely primordial."[37] And yet, "the monopolization of legitimate violence by the political-territorial association and its rational consociation into an institutional order is nothing primordial, but a product of evolution."[38] Weber suggests two forms of evolution, opposite sides of the same coin. The first of these is through the defense of a territory where, "arms are taken up by the members in the manner of a home guard."[39] This is the defense of the socio-economic and cultural manifestations of the daily lives of the defenders, be it families, crops, or holy sites. On the other side are "marauding raids" organized by "the most warlike members of the group."[40] These bands were centralized around a charismatic leader where the charisma manifested as physical prowess, courage, and a bit of luck. Their violence is also directed outward as the aggressive counterpart to the "home guard."[41] Legitimate internal violence, that is, violence directed within the territory at members of the same association, is another stage in the evolutionary process.

> Violence acquires legitimacy only in those case, however—at least initially—in which it is directed against members of the fraternity who have acted treasonably or who have harmed it by disobedience or cowardice. This state is transcended gradually, as this *ad hoc* consociation develops into a permanent structure.[42]

This internal violence also takes shape as a forming principle. Fratricidal violence is at the heart of many important formation myths.[43] Cain and Abel, along with Romulus and Remus, are fratricides that founded great cities.[44] Brutus's assassination of Julius Caesar should be understood as an attempt to restore the Roman Republic. Brutus's eventual death and the ensuing civil war between Octavian (later Caesar Augustus) and Mark Anthony establish the Roman Empire. Each of these, save for Cain and Abel, is an attempt to legitimize a certain way of being, namely a political order.[45] Fratricidal violence is also the basis of many modern political orders: the American War of Independence and the American Civil War certainly qualify as fratricidal and are contestations over legitimacy and authority. Violence, legitimacy, and authority are bound together in a mythological, sociological, and historical account of the State. If we compare Weber with Morris, a sociology of history against an ahistorical philosophizing of necessary elements, I suggest that Weber emerges as the better theory. Morris's targets of criticism (Rawls, Nagel, etc.), are similarly guilty of an over-reliance on philosophy, but maintain the historical reality of violence (or the threat of violence) as the historical reality of human political evolution.

Beyond the problem of history, Morris undervalues the power of the State. He says:

> [C]onsider what governments may do to motivate individuals without the threat of sanctions or force. States may prod by levying taxes or by imposing fees for different activities. They may also impose various restrictions or requirements on anyone wishing to carry out certain activities-for instance, licenses for those wishing to teach, to practice medicine, or to be a plumber, or insurance for anyone wishing to operate a motor vehicle or run a business. These may modify behavior and motivate without coercion or force (though they may violate rights to freedom).

Here, Morris fundamentally misunderstands the power of State coercion. State licensing restrictions do not prevent me (that is, violate my freedom) from offering my services on the free market. Yet, the reality is that if I do, and am discovered to be in violation of such laws, the power of the State will come down on me.[46]

Another thinker who keeps more on the historical side is Michel Foucault. His *Discipline and Punish* is central to any understanding of the modern penal system and, by extension, the most imminent apparatus of State coercion. Foucault's narrative traces the shift away from the punishment of the "body" in acts of torture to the punishment of the "soul."

> It might be objected that imprisonment, confinement, forced labour, penal servitude, prohibition from entering certain areas, deportation . . . are "physical" penalties: unlike fines, they directly affect the body. But the punishment-body relation is not the same as it was in the torture during public executions. The body now serves as an instrument or intermediary: if one intervenes upon it to imprison it, or to make it work, it is in order to deprive the individual of a liberty that is regarded both as a right and as property.[47]

The coercive power of State torture was magnified by the spectacle aspect. The grotesqueness of the punishments, each tailored to fit the crime like the damned in Dante's *Inferno*, was a teaching moment for the assembled crowds: *this* is the punishment for defying the State (usually in the person of the sovereign, hence the quotation attributed to Louis XVI: *L'état, c'est moi*). Other than lawyers and family members of the victims or the defendant, the only crowds which assemble for modern capital punishments are protesting for or against the act of execution. Yet these protests take place outside the walls of the prison, separating the individual defendant from the universal condemnation of capital punishment. Of course, some who protest capital punishment do so on a case-by-case basis, on grounds of police or prosecutorial misconduct, lack of direct evidence, or mental health concerns of the defendant. My point here is that the individual on death row is abstracted from the particulars of his crime by those who are against capital punishment per se, through the "hiddenness" of his person. Even lesser punishments are hidden behind the steel bars and barbed wire of the prison complex. Foucault notes, "Those who carry out the penalty tend to become an autonomous sector; justice is relieved of responsibility for it by a bureaucratic concealment of the penalty itself."[48] The closest to a spectacle in today's judicial system is the trial itself, before the necessity of punishment has even been decided. Deciding guilt or innocence is the spectacle of the modern world.[49]

Another historically grounded thinker, Charles Tilly, follows Weber's arguments concerning the monopolization of power at the heart of politics:

> [W]hatever else they do, governments organize and, wherever possible, monopolize violence. It matters little whether we take violence in a narrow sense, such as damage to persons and objects, or in abroad sense, such as violation of people's desires and interests; by either criterion, governments stand out from other organizations by their tendency to monopolize the concentrated means of violence. The distinction between "legitimate" and "illegitimate" force, furthermore, makes no difference to the fact. If we take legitimacy to depend on conformity to an abstract principle or on the assent of the governed (or both at once), these conditions may serve to justify, perhaps even to explain, the tendency to monopolize force; they do not contradict the fact.[50]

What, then, separates Alexander the Great from the pirate who dared challenge him? The answer should be "legitimacy," but the pirate's reply goes to the heart of the debate. What is legitimacy? How does it function in relation to sovereignty and authority? According to Tilly:

> Legitimacy is the probability that other authorities will act to confirm the decisions of a given authority. Other authorities, I would add, are, much more likely to confirm the decisions of a challenged authority that controls substantial force; not only fear of retaliation, but also desire to maintain a stable environment recommend that general rule.[51]

Tilly keeps to the Weberian concept of monopolized violence as the building block of legitimacy: "Eventually, the personnel of states purveyed violence on a larger scale, more *effectively*, more *efficiently*, with wider assent from their subject populations, and with readier collaboration from neighboring authorities than did the personnel of other organizations."[52] Here we encounter the concept of *assent*, though *consent* is used more often. Tilly makes an anachronistic claim here. To claim that consent is part of legitimacy is to beg the liberal values of democratic participation. The period Tilly is commenting on is the late medieval period, where assent would come from the nobility.

We are left with another grounding problem and perhaps another desacralization problem. Much like the other terms in this study, legitimacy is ambiguous. Legitimacy is "the justifications and acceptance" of "relationships of rule between governing authorities and individuals and communities,"[53] or "recognition of the right to govern."[54] Another possibility from Sadruski deals with consent:

> There is an important strand in liberal thinking that links legitimacy with the consent of the governed. Not the *actual* consent, of course, because such a requirement would undercut the whole search for the principles of political legitimacy; we would end up with the anarchistic idea that each individual is bound only by those laws to which he or she has agreed. . . . In a weak but plausible version, the liberal principle of legitimacy postulates that only laws that are based upon arguments and reasons to which no members of society have a rational reason to object can boast political legitimacy, and as such be applied coercively even to those who actually disagree with them.[55]

For Weber, legitimacy is a form of "self-justification."[56] It is also the degree to which the justification of authority works on the given populace. Legitimacy is not the same as authority since it comes later in the conceptual chain. If authority is raw power, then legitimacy is "reasoned" power in that the authority must convince its subjects to assent to its rule. Raw power can still be the basis for making a reasoned assessment to give assent and acknowledge legitimacy, but such brute power claims are dismissed in the liberal tradition; hence, Sadurski's appeal to other types of reason-giving. We can also return to Schmitt for an analysis of secularized legitimacy. The sacralized form of legitimacy is shown through the distortion of the illegitimate, or false, prophet. The false prophets of the Old Testament were illegitimate because they had not been given their message from God. God chooses, or legitimizes, Saul and David as kings of Israel. This transforms into the Divine Right of Kings (returning briefly to the *regnum* discussion in chapter 1). Once the despotisms of Europe fell, the legitimizing power is transferred to "the People," giving a deeper meaning to *vox populi vox dei*. Sovereignty and legitimizing power leave the same source (God) and migrate into the same source (the People). And yet, if my argument in chapter 1 is correct, that the People only possess a metaphorical and illusory sovereignty, is it necessary to say the same about legitimizing power? No, which only adds to the confusion. The myth of popular sovereignty is hidden by the myth of popular legitimacy. The metaphorical People (ideally any human, given the text of the American Declaration of Independence or the French Rights of Man) use the legitimizing power (usually in the form of elites) which they inherited from the philosophical debates of the seventeenth and eighteenth centuries to legitimize *themselves*. This circular track explains the difficulty in grounding legitimacy. Unlike authority which owes a great deal to (a show of) force, or sovereignty which requires the ability to declare the exception, legitimacy is fluid and fickle. A law or policy can be illegitimate due to a structural fault.[57] However, a government or particular official can go through the process of delegitimization by making a series of lawful but bad decisions that anger the populace. Because legitimacy is something granted apart from one's office (a president could become illegitimate, but the Office of the President would not), the People do have a role to play in how legitimacy plays out in a liberal democratic society. The People may not be sovereign, but they can certainly delegitimize those who anger them.

## SOLVING SCHMITT

One possible way to escape the democratic sovereignty conundrum in the proceeding sections is to redefine the meaning of exception to a broader context. The anti-monarchical tones of Enlightenment political philosophy and the positive portrayal of "the People" moved the locus of sovereignty into that collection of citizens.[58] By extending the political sphere beyond the blood nobility, the centrality of the sovereign begins to fade away. Sovereignty is weakened, but the problem of sovereignty (the exception, or the cliché "The buck stops here") is still unsolved. However, if sovereignty is weakened and then diffused into the civil service class, then the likelihood of exception can also be spread out. That is, exceptional circumstances a la Schmitt are less likely to occur as the possible problem faces multiple attempts to correct it. The State still holds the monopoly on violence, but as different aspects of the government coerce their targets differently, the monopoly is less clear.

A pre-modern diplomatic incident generally occurred between the main decision-makers in the situation (understanding that pre-electronic communication made the role of "ambassador" much more important than in the world of instant communication). The ambassador, who may have had an assistant in addition to a small secretarial staff, and the monarch with the members of the royal court, were the only actors who could diffuse or exacerbate a situation. "[T]he Enlightenment intellectuals . . . believed that the excesses of patrimonial bureaucracy, as part of the *ancien régime*, would disappear with the king, the royal court, and the nobility."[59] These predictions were obviously quite wrong. Now, the countries' foreign service apparatuses can be mobilized so that hundreds, if not thousands, of individuals are checking and double-checking every word of every statement or communique to make sure that linguistic nuance is correct, that the position taken aligns with the goals of the wider government and its allies, all while trying to get the other side to agree to whatever the demand was originally.[60] The exceptional crisis is waylaid by an army of bureaucrats. Of the individuals involved in solving the exception before it began, only two (in an American context, but no more than a handful in a European context) were actually elected: the president and vice president. It is to those bureaucrats, the anonymous sovereigns, to which I now turn.

## NOTES

1. An early draft of part of this chapter was presented at the Second Annual Political Theology Conference at Union Theological Seminary, October 2019. I am grateful to the participants for their insights and feedback.

2. Alan Wertheimer, *Coercion*, Studies in Moral, Political, and Legal Philosophy (Princeton, NJ: Princeton University Press, 2014), 13–14.

3. "Freedom" has its own definition in both fields, which adds to the difficulty of conceptualization.

4. Aristotle, *The Nicomachean Ethics*, trans. J. A. K. Thompson (New York: Penguin Books, 1976), 111; III. i.

5. Aquinas uses the term "simply" instead of "abstract" which is more philosophically correct but carries the complications of scholastic terminology. See Thomas Aquinas, *Commentary on Aristotle's Nicomachean Ethics*, trans. C. J. Litzinger, O.P. (Notre Dame, IN: Dumb Ox Books, 1993), 127–130.

6. Consider the late 2010s marketing campaign by Snickers, in which individuals are replaced by celebrities acting in extreme and humorous manners until they eat a Snickers, and by dealing with their hunger, return to normal. The tag line for the campaign was "You're not you when you're hungry."

7. This problem remains an aspect of the common law legal system: first-degree murder requires premeditation, while second degree murder is impulsive (in the moment) while still in a proper (i.e., not insane) frame of mind.

8. Albino Barrera, *Economic Compulsion and Christian Ethics* (Cambridge: Cambridge University Press, 2005), 6.

9. Wertheimer, 204. Emphasis original.

10. John Gardner, "The Many Faces of the Reasonable Person," *Law Quarterly Review*, no. 131 (2015): 563–584.

11. Wertheimer, 214.

12. See below on "reasonable alternatives."

13. Barrera, 9.

14. Joan McGregor, "Bargaining Advantages and Coercion in the Market," *Philosophy Research Archives* XIV (1988–1989): 27–28.

15. While implied, it should be noted that the negation (not do/not think) is also a possibility.

16. That is, A has the ability to help B with little to no risk to A. Pulling B out of a burning vehicle increases the odds of danger to A and necessarily complicates the "reasonable person" standard.

17. Unless A has a fiduciary duty toward B, but the thought experiment is designed to not imply this possibility.

18. In an instance where the coercer could perform the action directly, but coerces another to do it, it multiplies the difficulty in determining the ethics of the situation. I could clean up my children's rooms, that is I possess the capability to do so, but the importance of teaching responsibility comes into play. However, there could be situations in which there is no greater virtue/lesson being taught, and the coercer is merely manipulative or worse, sadistic.

19. Fictional literature gives examples of coercers who do not seem to fit this aspect. For example, the character of the Joker in the Batman comics and Oscar Wilde's Dorian Gray. Both men have passed desire for the sake of *something* to the desire for *anything* which will cure their boredom. It is the use of action without a goal that is the source of their disturbing fascination in popular culture.

20. Contra Miler who argues, "If we consider violence as essentially destructive, and lawful force as a civilized modification of violence, we may consider coercion as a further refinement of force characterized by virtual absence of any actual violence." William Robert Miller, *Nonviolence: A Christian Interpretation* (New York: Association Press, 1964), 37.

21. American Law Institute, *Restatement of the Law, Second, Contracts*, vol. 1, 3 vols. (St. Paul, MN: American Law Institute Publishers, 1981), §175, 475. Wertheimer makes reference to the original *Restatement*; I have chosen to use the updated text.

22. Wertheimer, 90. Emphasis original.

23. Ibid., 90–91.

24. This is an important caveat, as many blackmail situations come about through violations of privacy, trespass, or other criminal/ethically dubious acts.

25. Again, a caveat is necessary: If I had reason to believe the other individual involved was under the age of consent, I would have a legal/moral duty to inform the authorities.

26. This is not to say that sexual harassment cannot involve some degree of force, but that all forms of sexual assault do involve force, and thus a (crude) distinction can be made.

27. The comment by Harvey Weinstein's defense attorney, Benjamin Brafman, "Mr. Weinstein did not invent the casting couch," is a concession of the long-running practice of exchanging sexual favors for roles in Hollywood. The legal question in the Weinstein case is whether such a practice is consensual, and thus not sexual assault, or has *enough* elements of coercion/manipulation to reach the assault threshold in those situations where he is not being accused of outright rape. Part of the power of

the #MeToo movement is the exposure of the cultural and legal contradiction contained in the concept of "enough." Sexual assault is notoriously difficult to prove as a "consent" defense is always available to the defendant when the alleged incident takes place in private, and the victim's attempts to prove non-consent are thwarted by the cultural norms of the jury, which critics argue is akin to "victim-blaming." Also damaging has been political and media sensationalism of several high-profile rape accusations which were later proven to be false: the Duke Lacrosse case and the Rolling Stone article on the University of Virginia. On Weinstein, see James Queally, Richard Winton, and Hailey Branson-Potts, "Weinstein Cites 'casting Couch' Defense as He Faces Rape Charges in New York," latimes.com, http://www.latimes.com/local/lanow/la-me-ln-weinstein-case-20180526-story.html (Accessed August 11, 2018). On the Duke Lacrosse case, see Robert P. Mosteller, "The Duke Lacrosse Case, Innocence, and False Identifications: A Fundamental Failure to 'Do Justice'," *Fordham Law Review* 76 (2007): 1337–1412. On *Rolling Stone* see Sheila Coronel, Steve Coll, and Derek Kravitz, "Rolling Stone & UVA: Columbia School of Journalism's Report," *Rolling Stone* (blog), April 5, 2015, https://www.rollingstone.com/culture/culture-news/rolling-stone-and-uva-the-columbia-university-graduate-school-of-journalism-report-44930/.

28. In the sense that Aristotle claims adultery and murder are in *Nicomachean Ethics*. See Aristotle, Book II, vi.

29. This caveat removes the judiciary and most educators. The problem of public (higher) education as a part of the State was pointed out to me on at least one occasion by Matthew Day. I concede that merely separating higher education from the State as part of a thought experiment is not grappling with the complexities of being a part of that which I am critiquing, and my only reply is that, hopefully, this theoretical framework will enable others to apply it to particular interactions of the Academy and the State.

30. Though I am using terminology most applicable to the United States, any system in which power flows downward from a national (or supra/trans-national) framework would fit in the example.

31. Charles Tilly, "War Making and State Making as Organized Crime," in *Bringing the State Back In*, ed. Peter B. Evans, Dietrich Rueschemeyer, and Theda Skocpol (Cambridge: Cambridge University Press, 1985), 169.

32. Jonah Goldberg, *The Tyranny of Clichés: How Liberals Cheat in the War of Ideas* (New York: Sentinel, 2012), 81.

33. Romans 2:14–15.

34. Christopher W. Morris, "State Coercion and Force," *Social Philosophy & Policy* 29, no. 1 (January 2012): 34.

35. Ibid., 40–42.

36. Ibid., 40.

37. Weber, *ES*, 904.

38. Ibid., 904–905.

39. Ibid., 905.

40. Ibid.

41. Certainly, most of the members of the "home guard" are also those that would go on raids. Weber's reference to "the most warlike" should be understood as an ideal-type.

42. Weber, *ES*, 906.

43. By "myth," I mean stories which (real or not) serve to tell a group about themselves. The "myth" of Washington crossing the Delaware is "mythic" in that it communicates certain virtues (courage in the face of defeat) to all who see themselves in the narrative history of Washington.

44. Peter J. Leithart, *Defending Constantine: The Twilight of an Empire and the Dawn of Christendom* (Downers Grove, IL: InterVarsity Press, 2010), 329.

45. The text of Genesis 4 is unhelpful in establishing a motive for Cain's actions, other than the passing and unexplained claim that God did not favor Cain's sacrifice.

46. It could be argued that the misdemeanor charge and fine of several hundred dollars are far from the full power of the State. I agree with such claims. The problem is the possibility of ensuing non-compliance. See the previous quotation of Jonah Goldberg.

47. Michel Foucault, *Discipline and Punish: The Birth of the Prison* (New York: Vintage Books, 1995), 11.

48. Ibid., 10.

49. The decision-moment as spectacle overlaps with the current pop culture fascination of reality TV which has bled over into untraditional areas, such as Supreme Court decisions.

50. Tilly, 171.

51. Ibid.

52. Ibid., 173. Emphasis mine.

53. Steven Bernstein and William D. Coleman, "Introduction: Autonomy, Legitimacy and Power in an Era of Globalization," in *Unsettled Legitimacy: Political Community, Power, and Authority in a Global Era*, ed. Steven Bernstein and William D. Coleman (Vancouver, BC: UBC Press, 2009), 1.

54. Jean-Marc Coicaud, *Legitimacy and Politics: A Contribution to the Study of Political Right and Political Responsibility*, trans. David Ames Curtis (Cambridge: Cambridge University Press, 2002), 10.

55. Wojciech Sadurski, *Equality and Legitimacy* (New York: Oxford University Press, 2008), 27–28.

56. Weber, *ES*, 954.

57. In the legal setting of the United States, the determination of illegitimacy coincides with its cancellation (and authority, hence the confusion between the two concepts) at the order of the judicial branch.

58. Enlightenment views on "the People" harbored a great deal of elitism. Often, "the People" were those who were able to devote time to political discussion; "the Masses" were the "unthinking," "reactionary" part of the populace who were only concerned with their own short-term good.

59. "Introduction" in Glassman, Swatos Jr., and Rosen, 1.

60. This is clearly the case in escalating tensions between hostile states. War is certainly an exceptional state, even when there are laws controlling the manner and means in which wars may be declared and waged. Lincoln, Franklin Roosevelt, and George W. Bush each made decisions in the exceptional state that violated the rules/law, but the necessity of which is difficult to dispute within the historical context.

# 3

## Who Shapes the Shapers?

"If you're going to sin, sin against God, not the bureaucracy. God will forgive you but the bureaucracy won't."

—Admiral Hyman G. Rickover[1]

This chapter defines and analyzes the function of bureaucrats, especially in government service. I draw primarily from Weber's seminal work on bureaucratic systems. I also integrate aspects of the French postmodern movement (Foucault, Bourdieu) to add another dimension to Weber's system. Ultimately, I illustrate the ways in which bureaucracies use coercive power to assume the role of the sovereign.

Any discussion of bureaucracy necessarily calls Max Weber to the forefront. Weber's work on bureaucracy cannot be separated from his work on dominion and sovereignty. The move from traditional systems to modern, rational systems is only possible through the development of a highly organized bureaucratic class. Weber notes six "characteristics" or "functions" of bureaucracies: "jurisdictional areas," "office hierarchy," "written documents," "specialized office management," "full working capacity," and "general rules."[2] A few comments are necessary on each of these aspects, both in so far as they highlight the transition from pre-modern to modern systems and in the ways in which Weber approaches the central issues of the study.

The pre-modern administration of the "political community"[3] was handled by the chief or monarchy, the top advisors or royal court, and in larger systems, those who were indebted in some way to the chief/monarch.[4] These advisors (who existed in a patron/client relationship with the monarch) gave way to salaried positions, where the possibility of corruption in the patron/client system could be slightly mitigated, while also carrying "official duties."[5] More importantly,

> The authority to give the commands required for the discharge of these duties is distributed in a stable way and is strictly delimited by rules concerning the coercive means, physical, sacerdotal, or otherwise, which may be placed at the disposal of officials.[6]

The power of the bureaucracy is not innate to the structure, but is distributed or dispensed to the bureaucracy by the authority figure. The strict delimitation required a measure of permanency and specialization, which the older royal court model could not provide. Even the proto-bureaucracies of history are radically different from the modern ones.

> History shows that wherever bureaucracy gained the upper hand, as in China, Egypt, and to a lesser extent, in the later Roman empire and Byzantium, it did not disappear again unless in the course of the total collapse of the supporting culture. Yet these were still, relatively speaking, highly irrational forms of bureaucracy: "Patrimonial bureaucracies." In contrast to these older forms, modern bureaucracy has one characteristic which makes its "escape-proof" nature much more definite: rational specialization and training. The Chinese mandarin was not a specialist but a "gentleman" with a literary and humanistic education. The Egyptian, Late-Roman, or Byzantine official was much more of a bureaucrat in our sense of the word. But compared to the modern tasks, his were infinitely simple and limited; his attitude was in part tradition-bound, in part patriarchally, that means, irrational oriented.[7]

Weber also imposes a strict division between political leaders and bureaucrats.

> It is most important that the genuine official does not engage in politics, but "administers," above all *impartially*, as this is what his true vocation demands. It is crucial to remember this when assessing our former regime. The same principle applies to so-called "political" administrative officials as well. This, at least, is what his office requires, except where "reasons of state," i.e., the vital interests of the ruling order, are at stake. He should discharge his duties *sine ira et studio*, "without anger and partiality." He should not, then, do the very thing that politicians, leaders, or their followers, constantly and necessarily do: *fight*. Partisanship, struggle, passion—*ira et studium* [with anger and partiality]—are the element of the politician, and above all of the political *leader*. *His* conduct is governed by a principle of *responsibility* that is totally contrary to that of the official.[8]

I will return to this passage to unpack the meaning of "vital interests" and "responsibility." For now, it is enough to note that the ideal-type of both the politician and the bureaucrat requires a bifurcation not only between their roles but in their emotional responses as well. The neutrality of the bureaucrat (see below) is possible only through the lack of anger (for Weber), but this could be expanded to all emotional states.

Because coercive power is given to the bureaucracy, different levels of coercion are given to different levels of the office hierarchy. Likewise, the specialization and skill of the bureaucrats increase at the levels of the institution which are closest to the actual seat of power. The local office answers to the provincial office, which answers to the regional office, which answers to the national office, which answers to the international office. "Such a system offers the governed the possibility of appealing, in a precisely regulated manner, the decision of a lower office to the corresponding superior authority."[9] The difference between a structured system of appeal versus the pre-modern system is seen in the appeal of Paul to Caesar in Acts 25.[10] The Roman system allowed a citizen to appeal from a local governor directly to Caesar himself. The modern system (taking the United States' judicial system as the most direct comparison) would have at least three intervening bodies (appellate court, district appellate court, federal appellate court, Supreme Court). Only certain, time-sensitive issues can bypass the larger part of the system and go directly to the highest court.

It would be an error to understand Weber's insistence on the written nature of bureaucratic systems to mean simple recordkeeping. The compendiums of rabbinic commentary in the form of Talmud, Catholic canon law, Muslim *fatwa* collections, and the copious amount of material from Hellenistic Egypt illustrate the degree to which pre-modern systems were able to record and document important aspects of life.[11] Instead, Weber is referring to a *mindset*, a way of viewing the world, which strives for uniformity and consistency. A written bureaucratic document is a factual marker of history, "proof" that something was sold, a contract entered, or a wedding performed. If, for whatever reason, a bureaucrat is replaced, the next occupant of the office can read the written documentation or return to it when a question arises. The knowledge (and the authority which flows from that knowledge) is not innate to the bureaucrat (as *charisma* is in Weber's thought) but is held by the office (Weber's *institutionalization*).

The development of the bureaucratic system necessitated the development of managers to oversee the bureaucrats. Unlike a subsistence farmer who occupies multiple roles simultaneously, bureaucratic specialization required separating certain business functions from the actual bureaucrats. The pre-modern subsistence farmer had to be the employee, the bookkeeper, logistic coordinator, janitor, and so on. The bureaucrat in charge of overseeing the train systems of eastern Prussia could not be expected to also manage the maintenance of the office building. Bureaucracy requires the development of even more specialized functions in terms of administrative and support staff.

In contemporary terms, these functions run from human resource departments to custodial staff. The manager oversees her department but answers to a higher manager who oversees several lower managers. Herein lies the problem for democracies: "The bureaucratic hierarchy is controlled by an elite of top managers who make decisions with the technical advice, but without the consent of the below them in the hierarchy."[12] "The People" lack the technical knowledge to consent to most bureaucratic (and technocratic) decisions.

Weber's notion of "full working capacity" is another aspect of modern bureaucracies that is self-evident in the contemporary context. However, this was not the case in the pre-modern mindset. The king's advisors may have had a side job (likely in the education of nobles' children) to supplement their income. Their "area of concern" (to borrow a term from the academic world) could also shift depending upon the needs or whims of the monarch.[13] The specialization required by the modern bureaucrat generally, though not always, precludes a major shift in the area of concern.

## POPULAR CULTURE AND THE IMAGE OF THE BUREAUCRAT

Weber's bureaucrat seems like a fiction, given the common stereotypes found in the Anglo-American world of bureaucrats and bureaucracies. One place of difference is the perceived level of efficiency. In one sense, Weber's concern for efficiency is due to his relative temporal proximity (Germany's bureaucratization accelerated during Weber's professional life) and interest of non-bureaucratic systems of governmental rule. For Weber, the bureaucrat is characterized by specialization, that she is an expert in the subject matter under her purview. This is not the image that most of us have, especially in regard to governmental bureaucracies. Bureaucracy is often synonymous with "red tape," waste, and frustration. An early scene in the Disney/Pixar film *The Incredibles* is representative of the view of bureaucracy in pop culture. The scene shows Mr. Incredible's sense of his lack of purpose in order to set the plot in motion for the rest of the film. Yet it also contains several critiques of the stereotypical bureaucratic system. Mr. Incredible, as his alter-ego Bob Parr, works for an insurance company as part of the "supers" protection program, his true identity hidden from his co-workers. He dominates the space of his cubicle and desk, representing the one-size-fits-all mentality of the bureaucratic system. When faced with a clear injustice committed by his company, Mr. Incredible explains the convoluted system of forms and offices which will allow an elderly woman to be successful in her claim. Yet to avoid discovery, the two must act as though he has denied her request through exaggerated shouting and dramatic crying. Mr. Incredible's boss is a comically short man (Mr. Incredible is three times his size) who uses his authority to bully Mr. Incredible and prevent him from intervening in a mugging—until Mr. Incredible throws him through four walls.[14]

The difference between the specialized bureaucracy, in the sense of technical skill and knowledge, and the bureaucracy of the public perception is not a false difference. Generally, the average citizen does not need to interact with specialized bureaucrats.[15] These are the data analysis bureaucrats whose work only incidentally, if at all, reaches the public for consumption. In the previous example, Mr. Incredible is a data collection bureaucrat who must make decisions based on the comparison of that data to the pre-structured rules. The collection/analysis divide is apparent upon further analysis. The Census *Bureau* exists for a once-a-decade undertaking of *collecting* data on the American population.[16] Once that data has been collected and collated, it is used by other bureaucrats from the Department of Labor to Justice to congressional districting. The *analysis*, what the data *means*, is done by other bureaucrats who have their own rules and dictates to follow.

Beyond collection/analysis, bureaucracies also function to construct and deconstruct certain private/public divides. These divides are critical to the understanding of self. As Elshtain notes,

> Concepts like public and private constrain or enrich everyday life and activity. We are, each of us, shaped to and for a way of life whose public and private forms, linked to or embodied within a grammar of basic notions and rules, either strengthen or rob us of the power (*potentia*) to love and to work.[17]

The private/public divide takes many forms and is both historically and culturally conditioned.[18]

Weber shows an understanding of the intra-personal distinction in his depiction of the bureaucratic, reason-oriented modern political system, especially when compared to the pre-modern traditional and charisma-focused systems. Under the traditional systems, there was no divide between the ruler's public and private life. The capital the ruler controlled, whether it be economic, political, cultural, etc., could be gained and used in either category. The bureaucrat, bound as she is by the strictures of law and directive, has only public capital insofar as she is a bureaucrat. Her own skills and inter-office political gains are worthless, except in very unusual circumstances, outside of that very bureaucratic system. The favor she has curried with her superiors will not help her get a better deal on a car. Her superiors may recognize her as a friend and spend their own private social capital to assist, but not their public/bureaucratic capital. However, the deconstructive aspect of the public/private dichotomy is more important. The private citizen is forced to "go public" to the bureaucracy. Take, for instance, the Internal Revenue Service.

Businesses (both as a corporate "person" and the individuals who work in the business) are to track every expenditure, every receipt for tax purposes. From the perspective of the tax code, there is nothing inappropriate about a group of men having a business meeting at a less-than-"family-friendly" restaurant. Likely, neither the group of men who went to the restaurant which markets itself on having waitresses in less-than-professional clothing nor the woman who donated to Planned Parenthood Action Fund would want their conservative-leaning friends, co-workers, or family (especially their wives!) to have access to such information. Certainly, the IRS is not in a habit of revealing private information, but the nature of data is its permanency. Unless data is destroyed negligently, there is always the chance it can be revealed negligently, or with more nefarious intentions.[19]

If bureaucratic systems create private/public dichotomies, they are also capable of creating approved/disapproved categories. Bureaucracies function to channel the coercive power of their wider structure onto the individual. Coercion is the threat of and/or use of force to encourage or discourage a certain type of behavior and has long been recognized as the basis of political power. Law is coercion in that the possible violation of the statute carries the threat of force, contra James K. A. Smith, who calls laws "social nudges that make us a certain kind of people."[20] Twenty years in prison, much less capital punishment, is not a "nudge" but a life-defining (or ending) event. More so, limiting coercion to the field of behavior to acts of crime and violence hides the reality of social interaction. A lighthearted example is of the sports fan in the wrong town (e.g., the Red Sox fan living in New York). She can showcase her fandom through clothing, bumper stickers, and so on, and run the risk of being "alienated" from her community, or she can hide her fandom, watching the games in her home, and playing the part of supporting the home team. The not-so-lighthearted examples are simple to analogize: the "wrong" political/religious belief, the "wrong" race or ethnicity, the "wrong" sexual identity, and so on. In liberal states, the minority is protected from the worst forms of social and cultural coercion as the State coerces the majority on their behalf. The coercive power of Jim Crow laws in the Southern United States was (finally) displaced by the coercive power of Federal law in the form of antidiscrimination laws and regulations. Armed National Guard troops certainly helped as well.

However, it is Foucault's conception of the Panopticon, the all-seeing eye which regulates, manages, and controls the daily lives of the prisoners that has the most import for this discussion. The Foucaultian Panopticon is an institution that collects, organizes, and acts on data.[21] It is the bureaucratic regime of surveillance. But like the Orwellian prophecy of "Big Brother" (now reduced to a carefully edited reality TV show), the threat of the Panopticon is the belief-knowledge that it is always watching. Such a system can always watch everyone because everyone believes they are being watched because everyone is watching each other. The coercive power shapes behavior, even when the sovereign is not looking. The white and black speed limit signs are not merely a feature of safety but are a means of shaping the behavior of drivers, which is only magnified by red-light cameras.[22] Coercion-as-shaper is clearer the deeper into the bureaucratic system one looks. Both the penal and welfare benefit systems assume that their respective populations' "conduct must be closely supervised as well as rectified by restrictive and coercive measures."[23] The supervision of the convict occurs on his body through a complex scheme of surveillance both personal (the personal searches of both body and cell, required drug testing while on parole) and electronic (observation, monitoring while on parole). The welfare recipient is supervised by the bureaucracy in charge of social services, accompanied by the various forms and paperwork which are used to check whether the recipient has violated some aspect of the welfare "deal."[24] The threat of removal of benefits is another expression of the State's coercive power to dictate and shape behavior but in a carrot-and-stick manner. Not all Americans qualify for public assistance, but those who do qualify must regularly prove that they qualify. The benefit leads to another coercive regime. Those on welfare "find themselves the object of extensive record-keeping, constant testing, and close-up surveillance, allowing for the multiplication of points of restraint and sanction."[25] I will return to these problems in the following chapters.

Given the power and pervasiveness of bureaucratic systems, one could assume that more academic fields beyond Public Administration would be interested in understanding the dynamics of such systems. Strangely, the effects of the system, but not the system itself, receive attention. Consider the following:

> Surveillance has been coupled with the growth of the modern, bureaucratic state. The tools of the government to "know" and thus better care for and control its population have become more pervasive over time. These tools, such as the census, geographical survey, public health records, welfare rolls, voting register, national identity cards, passports, visas, etc., provide a statistical foundation of population management.[26]

The "tools" to "know" are equated with the bureaucracy. In this case, the bureaucracy is an arm of the State, controlled by the needs of the State. This is not an incorrect understanding of bureaucracy, but it is also too narrow. How and why the data is collected is subsumed into the mechanical tools of the State, hiding the agency of the bureaucracy as an institution and the bureaucrats as actors in the production of data. The complexities of the bureaucratic system, the interaction between rational-rules and the not-always-rational people who attempt to abide by them, is generally lacking across the various fields that take up the State as a matter of inquiry. Part of this hidden aspect of political life is due to the concept of bureaucratic neutrality.

> In some sense, the idea of neutrality can be seen in the practice thousands of years ago of rulers employing eunuchs to be in charge of their harems just as they hired professional accountants and auditors to manage their storehouses and treasuries.[27]

Eunuchs could manage the king's harem because there was no chance of the eunuch "stealing" the king's property. As bureaucracies moved toward the management of money, neutrality was dictated by the direct power of the ruler. Skimming from the monarch's treasury could result in losing one's head. Neutrality does not only apply "upward" but downward as well. The bureaucrat is expected to dispense her duties toward her "clients"[28] with the same neutrality. While some situations may evoke more of an emotional response, the bureaucrat is to leave those emotions for charity groups and to assess the situation of the client dispassionately. The dispassionate bureaucracy is criticized and ridiculed for being inflexible, but the true disaster for a bureaucratic system is when bias creeps into the system and grows so quickly that it becomes part of the "neutrality" of the system, to which I will turn in chapter 4.

I showed the progression of claims of sovereignty from early modern to the postmodern period in chapter 1. It ended with the paradoxical nature of sovereignty. No model of sovereignty can properly explain the place of "the People" in its calculus. Sovereignty, even in an elected body such as the United States Congress or the British Parliament, struggles under the weight of the Schmittian exception. The bureaucratic solution, in reality, was the League of Nations and later the United Nations on both the political and cultural fronts. Economically, the various G's (G7, G8, G20) along with the International Monetary Fund and the World Trade Organization implemented a bureaucratic approach to economic issues.[29]

## THE BUREAUCRAT/TECHNOCRAT DISTINCTION

While all bureaucrats have technical skills, few are in positions to dictate policies. In situations where they are able to, the bureaucrat becomes a technocrat. The technocrat represents the pinnacle of the bureaucratic hierarchy in that she goes from analyzing data to implementing the data in the most rational way possible.[30] The actualization of technical skill (colloquially called "experts") onto political systems creates a system in which the bureaucratic class becomes the dominant power in the system, at which point the term "technocrat" is most accurate.[31] Elections are transformed from a contest of charisma to a contest of policy implementations. A truly technocratic government would be difficult to hide; thus, my thesis should be equally difficult to defend. The bureaucrat is constrained or controlled by the rules which govern the bureaucratic system. The bureaucrat is as restricted by red-tape as the normal citizen, given that the function of the bureaucrat is to carry out their dictates as efficiently as possible. The technocrat is the bureaucrat who creates the systems, whether through administrative or regulatory diktat, or as advisors to the charismatic politicians who are not experts.

According to Weber,

> there are two diametrically contrasting types of domination, viz., domination by virtue of a constellation of interests (in particular: by virtue of a position of monopoly), and domination by virtue of authority, i.e., power to command and duty to obey.[32]

Yet Weber fails to comprehend the possibility of authority creating a feedback loop in which the two types of domination are not opposed, but collapse in on one another. This is the reality of technocratic systems in which a monopoly on power shapes the types of domination possible. Take, for example, the following:

> That public service in a democracy is a paradox has been and continues to be a central issue in public administration. Democracies cannot survive without a strong, technically competent, effective, efficient, and responsive public service, but the existence of such a public service contradicts the democratic notion of government by the people.[33]

The "public service" described is the epitome of Weberian ideal-type bureaucracy. The tension, or paradox, is between "the People" (or more precisely, the representatives of the People) who are prone to irrationality, inefficiency, and ineffective behaviors, and the bureaucracy, which is in control through their technical skill. This type of public service also embodies (in the ideal-type) political neutrality. The problem of democratic sovereignty is once again upon us.

One of the main "critics" of Weber's views on bureaucracy is Alasdair MacIntyre. Earlier, I referenced MacIntyre as a contributor to my thinking on how traditions (Christianity and modern liberalism) are conceptually held together. Here, however, I must part ways with MacIntyre's interpretation of Weber. Yet, MacIntyre's misreading of Weber is important insofar as it actually contributes to Weber's discussion of modernity. After briefly laying out MacIntyre's argument, I will suggest several ways in which Weber's concerns actually map onto parts of MacIntyre's concerns.

MacIntyre's *After Virtue* is a work which all ethicists must be in dialogue with, or at least have a response; one can disagree with MacIntyre, but he cannot be ignored. His controversial thesis is that the early modern period witnessed a shift in how ethical words are used: justice, right, and so on. MacIntyre allegorizes this as a dystopian future in which science is rejected, nearly eliminated, but then pieced back together in fragmentary forms, where the same words are used as before the rejection, but the meaning is radically disconnected from the previous tradition of "science" or completely wrong. MacIntyre's target of ire is the theory of emotivism, that all ethical statements are merely the speaker's opinion. "Good" means nothing more than "I like this" and "bad" means "I disapprove." But the terms "good," "bad," "justice," and "ought" are still used as if they appeal to an impersonal rationality or higher law. To say that murder is wrong seems to imply more than saying "I disapprove of murder."

MacIntyre argues that Weber's conception of the bureaucrat falls under this emotivist framework.[34] The structure of the bureaucratic class, especially the managerial class, acts as though certain claims to "correctness" are indeed true, but that the bureaucrats have no criterion on which to base their standard of correctness. More so, MacIntyre suggests that Weber advocated for this understanding of bureaucratic ethics. It is here that MacIntyre's argument falls flat on two points. Weber is describing the bureaucratic class, particularly of late nineteenth/early twentieth-century Germany, not constructing it. Weber works from historical sociology where normativity, if actually present, is the creation of the ideal-type from the various bits and pieces revealed by the historical undertaking. He works from the ground up, putting him in line with the great empirical traditions of philosophy. Thus, if Weber's project shows a strong case of emotivism in the bureaucratic managers, it would only help to bolster MacIntyre's claim of a modern shift in meaning, given the relations between modernity and the rise of the bureaucratic system.

The second problem for MacIntyre returns to the question of Weberian interpretation. Is modernity an "iron cage" which is good for humanity, bad for humanity, or a deterministic necessity? MacIntyre seems to read Weber as claiming modernity is a good, but as I noted above, I take Weber to be more cynical and actually troubled by the iron cage and modernity at large. The iron cage, whether it in itself is deterministic, has constrained the types of choices one can make. One is free to walk within the walls of the cage but not to transgress the boundary of it.[35] This, for Weber, is an unfortunate and tragic aspect of human development because there is no clear path through which humanity may continue on into more diverse systems of being and knowing. Creativity is impeded by the constant striving for efficiency and productivity while threatening the status quo of the system at hand. We are constrained by the walls of modernity (to which postmodern thought provides little to no help; the bars are polished and reflective but are still as impenetrable as before). On this reading of Weber, MacIntyre has more of an ally than a sparring partner.

Another critic of Weber, though limited to certain aspects, is Pierre Bourdieu. Bourdieu argues that Weber failed to take certain realities into consideration.

> The recognition of legitimacy is not, as Weber believed, a free act of clear conscience. It is rooted in the immediate, pre-reflexive, agreement between objective structures and embodied structures, now turned unconscious (such as those that organize temporal rhythms: viz. the quite arbitrary divisions of school schedules into periods).[36]

These unconscious recognitions of legitimacy are made in "immediate and tacit agreement, in every respect opposed to an explicit contract."[37] Legitimacy is not only a rational apprehension but an embodied experience of submission to the "legitimate" order.[38] Bourdieu turns to David Hume:

> Nothing is as astonishing for those who consider human affairs with a philosophic eye than to see the ease with which the many will be governed by the few and to observe the implicit submission with which men revoke their own sentiments and passions in favor of their leaders. When we inquire about the means through which such an astonishing thing is accomplished, we find that force being always on the side of the governed, only opinion can sustain the governors. It is thus solely on opinion that government is founded, and such maxim applies to the most despotic and military government as well as to the freest and most popular.[39]

Commenting on this passage from Hume, Bourdieu says:

> Hume's astonishment brings forth the fundamental question of all political philosophy, which one occults, paradoxically, by posing a problem that is not really posed as such ordinary existence: the problem of legitimacy. Indeed, essentially, what is problematic is the fact that the established order is *not* problematic; and that the question of the legitimacy of the state, and of the order it institutes, does not arise except in crisis situations. The state does not necessarily have to give orders or to exercise physical coercion in order produce an ordered social world, as long as it is capable of producing embodied cognitive

structures that accord with objective structures and thus of ensuring the belief of which Hume spoke-namely, doxic submission to the established order.[40]

Here Bourdieu is dealing, in his own way, with the problem not only of legitimacy but of sovereignty. "Crisis situations" certainly sounds like Schmitt's "exceptions." Yet Bourdieu is less concerned with who is sovereign and more with how that sovereignty is reinforced through lived structures. Sovereignty has "tricked" us into believing that it is "self-evident, as beneath consciousness and choice" when in reality it "has quite often been the stake of struggles and instituted only as the result of dogged confrontations between dominant and dominated groups."[41] This dominant/dominated bifurcation is a symbiotic (or parasitic) relationship. Any conception of sovereignty, power, or coercion creates the opposed categories of powerful/weak, secure/insecure, threatening/threatened.[42] But a simple bifurcation, though helpful, does not capture the complexities of power. The process of monopolizing violence is not between two groups, the powerful and the powerless, as the monopolization would have already been achieved. Instead, monopolization occurs on a continuum of power, from the most to the least, with various gradations between. Bourdieu simplifies the problem too far. Returning to the example of Charles II and the British Parliament, both had a certain type of power that each could exercise against the other. To say that one was "dominant" and the other "dominated" is nonsensical, until Charles lost all his power. This leads me to assert more strongly that the bifurcation should revolve around secure/insecure or threatening/threatened.

In such a diametric system, where does the bureaucrat fit? Given the theopolitical rhetoric of our historic moment, we could assume the bureaucrat represents the old guard, the conservative, or the status quo, due to the inertia of bureaucracies and is inherently connected to the first term in the above binaries. Such an assumption would be in error. Once again, political language is vague and unhelpful. The "conservative" does not conserve for the sake of conserving, just as the "progressive" does not progress for the sake of progressing. Both see some "good" (perhaps the most unhelpful political word of all) in how they approach political issues. Let us momentarily return to MacIntyre's misreading of Weber. The bureaucracy is amoral insofar as the issue of efficiency is concerned. Efficiency in carrying out the tasks of the bureaucracy is the "good" and its legitimacy comes from its "effectiveness."[43] The bureaucrat qua bureaucrat is less concerned by policy goals ("politics" in an Aristotelian sense) than by the application of those policies as efficiently as possible. The bureaucracy should have no affinity to a certain political party or outcome, as it is their job to implement the political will of the People as expressed through the representative system.

I have left the problem of popular sovereignty or "the People" unanswered. There are two ways, I suggest, of dealing with the problem. First, acknowledge the multivalent meaning of sovereignty, that Schmittian sovereignty is not what is expressed through popular sovereignty. This requires the additional step of differentiating and defining the locus of each type of sovereignty. The second way of dealing with popular sovereignty is to understand it as a "necessary fiction." I have adapted the idea of "legal fiction" (generally understood to be not-necessarily-true assumptions which facilitates the application of law) to one away from law (just as the Schmittian exception stands apart from the law) and toward its place in democratic society.[44] Even though we all "know" popular sovereignty is a fiction (even without ascribing to a Schmittian understanding), we carry on as if it were true on pragmatic grounds. The general stability of Western democracies has verified the utility of the fiction. Both of these options function similarly, though the second, in allowing the fiction to stand, allows for simplicity. Neither option changes in any real sense if representative democracy is replaced with participatory democracy or grassroots democracy.

I have illustrated the manner in which bureaucracies act as a conduit for State power. Part of the ubiquity of the bureaucratic problem is the way in which it reinforces these necessary fictions. We now move from the theoretical to the practical.

## NOTES

1. Linda Greenhouse, "Angry Dispute Left for New Senate," *The New York Times*, November 3, 1986, sec. II., B10.
2. Weber, *ES*, 956–958.
3. Ibid., 901.
4. The feudal system was, in modern parlance, a pyramid scheme in which duties and obligations were stacked upon each other as the system channeled downward. These duties and obligations were mediated by the closest authority figure. A peasant in modern Liverpool may have never seen, much less met, the English monarch. While the political theory dictated that the peasant was a subject of the monarch, the best way to demonstrate this was by serving the local lord or duke.
5. Weber, *ES*, 956.
6. Ibid.
7. Ibid., 1401.
8. Weber, *PV*, 173. Italics original to Weber, brackets original to the editors.
9. Weber, *ES*, 957.
10. See Peter van Minnen, "Paul the Roman Citizen," *Journal for the Study of the New Testament*, no. 56 (1994): 43–52 for an overview of the historical context.

11. On Hellenistic Egypt, see Giovanni B. Bazzana, *Kingdom of Bureaucracy: The Political Theology of Village Scribes in the Sayings Gospel Q*, Bibliotheca Ephemeridum Theologicarum Lovaniensium, CCLXXIV (Leuven, Belgium: Peeters, 2015).

12. Glassman, Swatos, and Rosen, 2.

13. This transition has not completely departed from the modern system: ministerial cabinets of European parliamentary countries often change portfolios. This is nearly unheard of the American system, certainly in the same administration. This highlights one of the major differences between the American and European models; American Cabinet members are not elected as the majority of European parliamentary ministers are.

14. Brad Bird, *The Incredibles*, DVD (Pixar/Walt Disney Studios, 2004).

15. Judith E. Gruber, *Controlling Bureaucracies: Dilemmas in Democratic Governance* (Berkley, CA: University of California Press, 1987), 1–2.

16. While the Census Bureau does do more than merely prepare for and execute the census, the Constitutional requirement gives this bureau its central purpose as part of the Department of Commerce.

17. Jean Bethke Elshtain, *Public Man, Private Woman: Women in Social and Political Thought* (Princeton, NJ: Princeton University Press, 1981), xiv.

18. Ibid., 4.

19. On the former, see Alan Rappeport, "Up to 100,000 Taxpayers Compromised in Fafsa Tool Breach, I.R.S. Says," *The New York Times*, January 20, 2018, sec. U.S., https://www.nytimes.com/2017/04/06/us/politics/internal-revenue-service-breach-taxpayer-data.html (Accessed September 24, 2018), on the latter, the breach of the Democratic National Committee emails in the months leading up to the 2016 presidential election is the quintessential example.

20. James K. A. Smith, *Awaiting the King: Reforming Public Theology* (Grand Rapids, MI: Baker Academic Press, 2017), 10.

21. As opposed to the Benthamite Panopticon, which is a literal space in a prison, I refer to the Foucaultian Panopticon in its metaphorical sense.

22. Here we see another example of the ideal type versus reality; it is unsafe to go the posted speed limit on I-75 through Atlanta (55 mph) because of all the other cars going 70 to 80 mph.

23. Loïc Wacquant, *Punishing the Poor: The Neoliberal Government of Social Insecurity* (Durham, NC: Duke University Press, 2009), 79.

24. Ibid., 50.

25. Ibid., 106.

26. Mark B. Salter, "Surveillance," in *The Routledge Handbook of New Security Studies*, ed. J. Peter Burgess (New York: Routledge, 2010), 193. I take up parts of the issue of surveillance in chapter 4.

27. Gerald E. Caiden, "The Concept of Neutrality," in *Democratization and Bureaucratic Neutrality*, ed. Halie K. Asmerom and Elisa P. Reis (London: Palgrave MacMillan, 1996), 21.

28. The terminology is Gruber's.

29. Which will be discussed in greater detail in chapter 4.

30. Recall Weber's ideal-type.

31. I will use this distinction between bureaucrat/technocrat throughout.
32. Weber, *ES*, 943.
33. Mary R. Hamilton, "Democracy and Public Service," in *Democracy and Public Administration*, ed. Richard C. Box (Armonk, NY: M.E. Sharpe, Inc., 2007), 3.
34. MacIntyre, *After Virtue*, 26.
35. This is the illusion of choice, when in reality the choices have been narrowed down by unseen factors.
36. Bourdieu, "Rethinking," 14.
37. Ibid.
38. Recall Tilly's arguments on legitimacy.
39. David Hume, "On the First Principles of Government," cited in Bourdieu, "Rethinking," 15.
40. Bourdieu, "Rethinking," 15.
41. Ibid.
42. In applying these types of binaries to concrete phenomena, Wacquant suggests a "liberal-paternalist" approach occurs in neoliberal states, that is "permissive at the top, with regard to corporations and the upper class," while being "authoritarian" toward those at the bottom. See Wacquant, 8.
43. MacIntyre, *After Virtue*, 26.
44. Lon Fuller, *Legal Fictions* (Stanford, CA: Stanford University Press, 1967), especially 17–19.

# 4

## Bureaucracy Ascendant

This chapter focuses on concrete examples of the combination of bureaucracy and coercion while adding and acknowledging a third aspect—neoliberalism. I contend that neoliberalism is the fulfillment of the "iron cage" of modernity through its ability to constrain and coerce all aspects of human life. The synergistic nature of bureaucratic coercion and neoliberal thinking creates a troubling nexus—a Scylla and Charybdis situation—in which a society *may* be able to sail the narrows but is more likely to fall into disaster. This chapter has four major sections: (1) a historical account of neoliberalism, (2) an analysis of gender and the bureaucratic-neoliberal nexus, and (3) an analysis of race and the bureaucratic-neoliberal nexus, and (4) an analysis of public health rhetoric and responses to the COVID-19 pandemic.

Neoliberalism, as a point of academic interest, has rapidly grown since the 2008 Great Recession. Academic investigations of neoliberalism have moved beyond the "purely" economic matters into other areas of human existence. Part of the interest in neoliberalism is its apparent resiliency. The two previous economic collapses, the Great Depression of the late 1920s through World War II, and the inflation crisis of the mid- to late 1970s, each produced a change in the prevailing economic systems. The 2008 crisis instead saw a doubling-down on the previous economic model.[1]

But what is neoliberalism, and what does it have to do with my claims of sovereignty, bureaucracies, and coercive power? At times, neoliberalism seems to be a catch-all term for late twentieth/early twenty-first century capitalism. Consider the following eight-point definition:

1. A confidence in the market as an efficient mechanism for the allocation of scarce resources.
2. A belief in the desirability of a global regime of free trade and free capital mobility.

3. A belief in the desirability, all things being equal, of a limited and non-interventionist role for the state.
4. A conception of the state as a facilitator and custodian, rather than a substitute for market mechanisms.
5. A defense of individual liberty.
6. A commitment to the removal of those welfare benefits that might be seen as disincentives to market participation (in short, a subordination of the principles of social justice to those of perceived economic imperatives).
7. A defense of labor market flexibility and the promotion and nurturing of cost-effectiveness.
8. A confidence in the use of private finance in public projects and, more generally, in the allocative efficiency of market and quasi-market mechanisms in the provision of public goods.[2]

The popular image of bureaucracy (explored in chapter 2) is often used as the foil against neoliberal ideas. Points (3) and (4) certainly go against most notions of bureaucratic power and seem to contradict my theory of coercion. Yet, in these eight points, "efficiency" or its cognates appear three times with another two points implying it to a degree. Weber suggests that bureaucracies are only truly possible with the advent of capitalism, and thusly we should expect more developed bureaucracies as more developed capitalism emerges. There is also bureaucratic tension between (3) and (4). The State should not intervene but should always be vigilant to intervene to keep the system running.

Historical investigations of neoliberalism vary, though not nearly as much as the ideological investigations, as illustrated below. Most scholars place the "arrival" of neoliberalism in the 1980s under the Thatcher-Reagan administrations and often begin their investigations there. Mitchell and Fazi go a generation back and explain the precursor systems which allowed for neoliberalism to take hold. These include the bastardization[3] of Keynesianism and the "contradictions inherent in the Bretton Woods arrangements."[4] The Bretton Woods system had established the United States as the standard international currency due to it being the only developed economy relatively unscathed by World War II. While the details are unnecessary for this study, the Bretton Woods arrangements contained the seeds to the inflation crises of the 1970s and its own demise.[5] Quinn Slobodian goes even further back, to the aftermath of World War I, with thinkers such as von Mises and Hayek.[6]

Critiques of neoliberalism are more common among left-wing thinkers, especially from various schools of Marxism.[7] Marxist critiques are especially illuminating when targeting the supposed "value-neutral" and "natural" designations of neoliberalism as an economic model. The overlapping field of Critical Studies expands the economic critique into other areas.

> It is impossible to define neoliberalism purely theoretically, for several reasons. First, methodologically, although neoliberal experiences share important commonalities . . . neoliberalism is not a mode of production. Consequently, these experiences do not necessarily include a clearly defined set of invariant features, as may be expected in studies of "feudalism" or "capitalism," for example. Neoliberalism straddles a wide range of social, political and economic phenomena at different levels of complexity. Some of these are highly abstract, for example the growing power of finance or the debasement of democracy, while others are relatively concrete, such as privatisation or the relationship between foreign states and local non-governmental organisations (NGOs). Nevertheless, it is not difficult to recognise the beast when it trespasses into new territories, tramples upon the poor, undermines rights and entitlements, and defeats resistance, through a combination of domestic political, economic, legal, ideological and media pressures, backed up by international blackmail and military force if necessary.[8]

Under this interpretation, neoliberalism is not merely an economic arrangement but a fully developed, self-sustaining, political, cultural, and moral system. Or, as Wendy Brown claims in her *Undoing the Demos*:

> [N]eoliberalism assaults the principles, practices, cultures, subjects, and institutions of democracy understood as rule by the people. And more than merely cutting away the flesh of liberal democracy, neoliberalism also cauterizes democracy's more radical expressions, those erupting episodically across euro-Atlantic modernity and contending for its future with more robust versions of freedom, equality, and popular rule than democracy's liberal iteration is capable of featuring.
>
> The claim that neoliberalism is profoundly destructive to the fiber and future of democracy in any form is premised on an understanding of neoliberalism as something other than a set of economic policies, an ideology, or a resetting of the relation between state and economy.[9]

And yet, I have shown previously that the bureaucratic mindset, expressed most clearly through efficiency and coercion, has already undermined the very structures which Brown seeks to defend. The ideal-type bureaucrat in Weber is the ideal-type bureaucrat in neoliberalism.[10] To fully illustrate this claim, I will turn to Adam Kotsko's *Neoliberalism's Demons* and his mild critiques of Brown before putting forward my concerns with both works.[11] The following examples should be understood as a (perhaps *the*) case study into the ways bureaucratic systems have become so ubiquitous that even those systems which claim to be opposed to bureaucratic interference actually require the coercive power that bureaucracies enable.

Brown argues that neoliberalism shifts the apex of human life from a communal, political sphere to the individualized, economic sphere.

> [N]eoliberal reason, ubiquitous today in statecraft and the workplace, in jurisprudence, education, culture, and a vast range of quotidian activity, is converting the distinctly political character, meaning, and operation of democracy's constituent elements into economic ones. Liberal democratic institutions, practices, and habits may not survive this conversion.[12]

While Kotsko presents a compelling counter-argument to Brown's bifurcation of the political/economic, she is onto something very Weberian with her notion of "neoliberal reason" and its expansion into realms not traditionally associated with economics. Indeed, a Weberian "genealogy" of capitalism would suggest as much. If the spirit of capitalism is best expressed through the Protestant (especially Calvinist) ethic of attempting to find security in the face of God's sovereignty expressed through predestination, as Weber claims, it is also the fact that the secularization of that ethic allowed it to be expropriated to other areas of life. If the predestination/sovereignty of God is removed (secularized) from the ethic which birthed capitalism, its bindings to that original context are also undone. Capitalist reason is exported from the corporation to other areas of non-economic life through the efficiency of the bureaucratic regime. Pragmatically, bureaucratic efficiency works by streamlining and simplifying all those aspects of the job which can be reformed. Once the trade-offs in the process of efficiency-maximization are identified, it is not surprising that other sectors (both physically, as forms of production, or mentally, as the development of a mindset) would attempt to replicate similar successes. The rule-based system of bureaucratic thinking allows for measurable standards and objective goals. This is clearly seen in the field of K-12 schooling, with an emphasis on standardized testing and benchmarks for students to meet.[13] Perhaps more troubling is the expansion of neoliberal thinking into areas that have traditionally been the domain of ethics and sociology. Kotsko analyzes the Nobel Lecture of economist Gary Becker, in which Becker applied economic rationality (cost-benefit analysis, price points, etc.) to non-economic concepts like racism and criminality. Kotsko notes:

> In the first case [racial discrimination], taking for granted that some people have racist preferences, Becker argues that such preferences may not be absolute and hence could be offset by higher costs in other areas—whether through legal sanction in the case of antidiscrimination laws or through the less direct path of

providing high-quality job training to minorities to make their value as employees outweigh the benefit the racist believes he derives from discrimination against them. In other words, the goal of public policy should be to figure out how much racial discrimination is really worth to people and the either make it unaffordable or else make nondiscrimination too profitable to pass up.[14]

This ego-utilitarian ethic is problematic in a number of respects. The notion of hating some aspect of another person but holding that aside as long as they are useful to one's self implies a return (or at least, the possibility of return) to that hatred once the other's usefulness has "run-out." Such an ethic is diametrically at odds with the ethics of Jesus, who commanded that his followers love those who could not be useful to them (the Parable of the Good Samaritan). Additionally, Becker's other proposal, increasing antidiscrimination law, must be viewed through the lens of coercion. Coercing the southern states into ending racist policies did not undo the non-government forms of racism. If anything, this type of coercive power may increase the individual's racism. This does not mean that coercion cannot or should not be a part of public policy, merely that the application of coercion does not necessarily follow the rationality of a Nobel economist.

While these and other forays into non-economic spaces would be an interesting study, the key bureaucratic system I wish to discuss in relation to neoliberalism is international monetary policy and loans. There are a number of different organizations that fall under this system with multiple points of overlap. As a shorthand to identify these groups, I will refer primarily to the International Monetary Fund (IMF) and the World Bank.[15] These respective institutions are the epitome of bureaucratic and unelected coercive power, even as both organizations attempt to clothe themselves in the legitimacy of democratic participation:

> The IMF/World Bank and WTO gain their legitimacy as *political* entities set up to direct and regulate a global economy; by their very existence, they counter the logic of pure capitalism. The organizations draw on a rhetoric of international democracy built through consensus and participation. They claim to provide a supranational forum for global public deliberation.[16]

The logic of "pure capitalism" is the admixture of points 3 and 4 in the definition of neoliberalism above. The State should get out of the way to allow the market to work, but the State must be involved enough so that the market can work. The sui generis nature of the Market has been deconstructed by a number of thinkers and theories over the past half-century. But these institutions also have an internal methodology that exists beyond the reach of "global public deliberation" as a neoliberal ideological consensus was forged within the main intergovernmental organizations at the center of the contemporary system of economic governance: the meetings of the G7 finance ministers, the International Monetary Fund, the OECD, and the Bank for International Settlements.[17]

The ideological commitments to neoliberalism belie the notion of democratic participation. Instead, their "resiliency" in the face of the 2008 Financial Crisis is due to "a combination of international competitive and coercive pressures" which "have led to a deepening of networks of cooperation between national monetary authorities and have propelled this increasingly transnational monetary authority to the heights of the 'new international financial architecture.'"[18] Though individuals are unable to access these institutions, that does not mean that their coercive power cannot reach the level of the average citizen.

Both the IMF and the World Bank were formed as part of the larger Bretton Woods framework. Originally, the World Bank dealt with development loans while the IMF focused on monetary exchange rates based on the American Dollar. After Nixon removed the Dollar as standard, international exchange rates went to a "floating" system and the IMF had lost its institutional purpose. The IMF reestablished itself as having some similar functions with the World Bank while providing advanced "technical" support to developing countries. As part of receiving loans, countries would have to meet certain thresholds which indicated a likelihood of repayment. Returning to the discussion in chapter 2 of the difference between coercion and offer, it seems at first glance that loans are offers. In an individual or small-business loan that is certainly the case. The penalties for defaulting are part of the nature of the otherwise legal and fair framework of the loaning system, leaving aside for the moment the issues of "payday" loans and predatory lending practices. In fact, one can "shop" for the lowest loan rates among different financial institutions, a natural aspect of an offer. It is farcical to imagine going to another mob boss and trying to get a better "coercive offer" than the original threat.

What makes loans from the IMF and World Bank different than an individualized loan, other than the size? First, these groups hold a monopoly on loans of the scale needed by developing countries. The ability to freely "shop" is greatly diminished when there are only two open stores, both of which operate on the same fundamental principles. Second, loans to developing countries are not like an individual taking out a loan to remodel her bathroom. Especially in the context of the 2008 Financial Crisis, these loans function more like the at-best-questionable payday loans mentioned previously, as many political leaders see turning to these institutions as a necessity, regardless of the political risks.[19] Yet neither of these elements, separate or combined, rises to the level of moral coercion. The transformational element is the requirement of disrupting state sovereignty. The IMF and World Bank require countries to meet certain benchmarks *before* receiving a loan, usually requiring austerity measures. The perspective of these institutions is that the borrowing country needs to prove the capacity to pay back the loans. If the borrowers continue with similar behavior that created the financial crisis in their country, loaning money would merely fix the superficial symptoms of the problem rather than providing a cure. Individual loans often require proof of the likelihood of repayment, but not to the extent that the bank forces a change to one's lifestyle. To put this back in Schmittian terms, at the exceptional moment of a financial crisis, the sovereign uses her extra-legal status to surrender it to the World Bank or IMF. The act of sovereignty becomes the undoing of sovereignty as it is transferred, at least in the financial realm, to a committee of technocrats.

During the high point of World Bank/IMF intervention in the financial crises of the 1970s, the range of available options was wide for these technocrats.

> In exchange for their assistance, the World Bank and IMF imposed strict economic policies, known as Structural Adjustment Programs, on the developing countries. The SAPs are in keeping with the mainstream macroeconomic policies that have been found to be successful in the Western democracies over the past five decades. The major SAP components include reductions in government spending; a tightening of government monetary policy; currency devaluation (typically against the hard currencies such as the US dollar); reductions in barriers to trade, including import tariffs and quotas and controls on foreign investment; privatization of government-owned enterprises; market deregulation (especially with respect to price ceilings and wage floors); and a focus on the production of exports in which the developing country has a comparative advantage.[20]

Some of these are quasi-coercive in that they produce short-term (in theory) harmful effects for long-term gain (such as a reduction in government spending). Others are more difficult to classify as coercive (focus on competitive exports). What the World Bank/IMF missed that this passage picks up on is the cultural and social structure of Western democracies that may be radically different from embryonic democracies with a different socio-cultural makeup in other parts of the world. Yet, there is a noted tension between the coercive effects of the World Bank/IMF and its success in creating change. The possibility for extreme coercion is always present, but the political nature of the real-world checks that threat.

> When they [the IMF and World Bank] work with governments, their influence is in part persuasive and in part coercive. They can lend, catalyze other lending, or indeed stop lending. Equally, they can define, impose, and monitor tough

> conditionality on borrowers. This gives them obvious bargaining power. But the record of failed conditionality reveal that borrowing governments seldom actually do as they are told. The power to enforce conditionality by withholding money or the like can be easily dissolved by powerful political pressures to continue lending. Equally, the institutions sometimes have their own reasons for not enforcing conditionality, such as to ensure repayment of their loans. This puts an emphasis on a more subtle, persuasive kind of influence.[21]

Economic coercion can have more unintended consequences on a global scale than other types of coercive conditionality. But what strikes deepest at the colloquial notion of sovereignty in these situations often takes an ironic flair.

> Compliance is painful, especially when costs are front-loaded and benefits are deferred. Powerful special interests will inevitably be opposed. Even focusing on key reforms central to the borrower's ability to restore economic growth and, at the same time, to exit its Fund program—the two obviously legitimate goals of conditionality—is easier said than done. Strengthening the police, judiciary, and tax administration, for example, will be priorities for an IMF that believes economic growth depends on rule of law, but laying off judges, policemen, and tax administrators may be necessary to balance the budget and ensure that the Fund is repaid at the end of three years.[22]

In countries where the government is the main employer, shrinking the government payroll has a ripple effect on the weaker private sector as their main consumers are now out of work.[23] Efficiency turns in on itself and becomes grossly inefficient by undercutting the private sector which it is supposed to support. Even in countries not facing the coercive remaking of their economies, the relationship between the private and public sectors is tenuous. Bourdieu explores this relationship through a multilayered metaphor of the "right" and "left hands" of the state.[24]

The most interesting, but also the most debatable, explanation for this metaphor is the Euro-America right/left political divide. The evidence for such a reading comes from the grouping of professions ("minor civil servants," "policemen, lower-level judges, social workers, educators") who "feel abandoned if not disowned outright, in their efforts to deal with the material and moral suffering that is the only certain consequence of this economically legitimated Realpolitik."[25] The right/left stereotypes of business-friendly (capital) versus worker-friendly (labor) are packed into Bourdieu's division. The other, and perhaps more obvious reading, is as an allusion to Matthew 6:3—"But when you give to the poor, do not let your left hand know what your right hand is doing." Yet Bourdieu inverts the order in that these social professions "experience he contradictions of a state whose right hand no longer knows, or worse, no longer wants what the left hand is doing," so that the left hand is the one attempting to help the poor while the right hand is ignorant or, in Bourdieu's formulation, actively opposed to the goals of the left hand.[26] While Bourdieu may not go this far, I think it can be said that the right hand of government does have genuinely admirable goals it is trying to actualize. The tension between the two hands seems to be a matter of resource allocation—but it may be, in fact, a matter of mindset. Here, we make the turn to neoliberalism and bureaucracy.

## BUREAUCRATIZATION OF BODIES

Bodies are, for good or ill, categorized according to certain biological, physiological, and cultural notions. One of the key aspects of human culture is the creation and maintenance of these (and other) categorical lines. This is a critical contribution to human understanding from thinkers like Émile Durkheim and Mary Douglas.[27] Classificatory schemes exist to make sense of the world. For the first two examples, gender and race, the categorizations are deeply embedded into the American psyche. Even though bureaucratic systems rely on categorization, many of these categories pre-date the development of any bureaucratic regimes. The categorization of humans is not necessarily the result of any of the other issues at play in this study. Just as with those issues, we cannot make a pronouncement on the rightness or wrongness of individual categories until they are placed in context.

There are two aspects to the bureaucratization of bodies: knowledge and control. The two aspects are linked in a chicken-and-egg paradox: to know requires control, but to control requires knowledge. If one can be separated from the other conceptually, it is better to say that knowledge comes before control. Knowledge can be partial and still meaningful; partial control may be no control at all. Thus, I turn first to the concept of knowing persons.

The knowing-of-persons is best expressed through the concept of privacy or the not-knowing-of-persons. Usually, privacy is contraposed with surveillance which, while accurate, carries too much baggage from the military/police framework. As an example, it seems incorrect to say that advertising companies are "surveilling" my shopping habits, especially when I willingly share it in return for discounts. However, my data is used in both aggregate (demographics broken down by age, gender, etc.) and targeted ways. The problems with the term surveillance lead me to embrace (and slightly modify) the vocabulary used by Sarah Igo in her book *The Known Citizen*.[28] The "known" individual has come into contact with institutions and organizations whose mission is to collect and analyze data, whether public institutions or private companies. A "knowing" society is one that attempts to create these contacts.

> Even as Americans grasped at wider freedoms in the twentieth century they . . . were becoming ever more intelligible to an expanding array of parties: state bureaucracies and law enforcement; the popular press and marketers; financial institutions and private corporations; scientific researchers and psychological experts, and, eventually, data aggregators and proprietary algorithms. A knowing society impinged on individual liberties in unsettling ways. Being known could bring punishment from the state or destroy a reputation crafted for peers; it could raise one's insurance rates or cost someone a job. It could even compromise one's free will and sense of authentic personhood.[29]

The pairs in this passage are illustrative. Igo links the notion of state bureaucracies with state power ("law enforcement" and "punishment"). Interestingly, though she has no sustained comments on bureaucracy or Weber, Igo gestures toward Weber's concerns about the constriction of human choices. Recall the discussions in chapters 2 and 3 regarding the public/private divide created by bureaucratic systems. These are necessary to the proper working of the State; that is, the *polis* requires some element of the citizens' lives to be public.[30] The public/private dichotomy is not an either/or in which one is either *fully* public or *fully* private. Instead, the struggle for individual citizens is to navigate the subtleties and nuances between what information is partially public and partially private. The problem is that citizens have little to no control over their information once it is in possession of a bureaucratic system. Increasingly, there is little of the private citizen left.

To explore this issue, I will turn to the welfare system as a symbol of this bureaucratic power. This is not a critique of any particular public policy decision; just like our bureaucratic subjects under discussion, the policy positions are less important than having a policy. In fact, by going a step deeper than the policy debates, we can analyze how the bureaucratic mindset of the welfare state affects the individuals in its care. But we must also be aware that the welfare state plays out through gendered conceptions.[31] The pejorative "Welfare Queen" rhetoric resonated due to popular imagination and cultural expectations of welfare.

The American welfare state emerged in the wake of the Great Depression and Roosevelt's "New Deal" policies. The longest-lasting of these initiatives is Social Security Insurance, which established the quintessential marker of bureaucratic recordkeeping, the Social Security number. This nine-number sequence became the most efficient way of identification in America as (1) all citizens were to be assigned a number at birth or naturalization and (2) the sequence was unique to each individual. Names and dates of birth could be identical, but similar to a paper version of a fingerprint, the SSN was one-of-a-kind. One of the most important aspects of a Social Security number is access to benefits at either the state or federal level.

One of the most politically contested public benefits operates under the general rubric of "welfare." Here, welfare is a catch-all term referring to those programs that are designed specifically to assist those whose incomes are near or below the federal poverty level. Welfare is a needs-based system in which the applicant must show they fall into the income range for the benefit in question. Naturally, a bureaucratic system was established to handle applications, check for instances of fraud, and facilitate payments or other benefits to those who qualified. As American economic prosperity fluctuated with low points in the late 1970s and post-2008 and with a relative high point in the mid-1990s, so did the political nature of the programs.

Loïc Wacquant's *Punishing the Poor* is a provocative account of the growth of the American prison system post-1970s *and* the transformation of the American welfare system in the mid-1990s. It is a fascinating account of the interaction between neoliberal thinking and policies that shape American life. In this section, I will analyze his account of the 1996 welfare reform and draw out the ways the bureaucracy is instrumental in actualizing the changes.

According to Wacquant, the Personal Responsibility and Work Opportunity Reconciliation Act of 1996 (PRWORA)[32]

> was never meant to fight poverty and alleviate social insecurity; on the contrary, it was *intended to normalize them,* that is, to inscribe them as modal experience and accepted standards of life and labor for the new service proletariat of the dualizing metropolis, a task which is indivisibly material and symbolic. It was the culmination of a train of measures deployed over the preceding two decades whereby the American state has turned away from passively protecting the poor toward actively making them into *compliant workers, fit or forced to fill the peripheral slots* of the deregulated labor market.[32]

Wacquant likely goes too far in ascribing nefarious intentions to otherwise good-faith actors (or at least, bipartisan[33]) and borders on giving agency to an idea-system (which itself borders on the pejorative meaning of conspiracy theory). However, for the sake of argument, I will take his description of the effects on the American system as correct. This includes his description:

> Several features of the overhaul of public aid at century's close both mirror and complement the workings of penal and caste hierarchies; the built-in gender slant; the practical presumption that recipients of welfare are "guilty until proven innocent" and that their conduct must be closely supervised as well as rectified by restrictive and coercive measures; and the deployment of deterrence and stigma to achieve behavioral modification.[34]

Such a system requires a bureaucratic system to "supervise" and "rectify," not only at the point of contact between the individual and the State (the welfare office or its variations in such areas as job placement) but also at the higher levels of government to create the rules and procedures the bureaucrats are to follow to achieve these outcomes.

The gendered aspect of this system can be seen in the statistics. Narrowing in on the "Temporary Assistance for Needy Families" (TANF) program, more than five times the number of female adults to male adults receive aid.[35] As this program was designed to target children, the connection between single motherhood and poverty is apparent.[36] Points of connection can expand into other areas, multiplying the difficulties for these women. Single mothers are less likely to have a college degree, limiting their employment opportunities. This is Wacquant's main point on PRWORA as an outworking of neoliberalism. In achieving the seventh aspect of our working definition of neoliberalism (removal of disincentives to work), it contributes to the eighth aspect (flexible labor) and to which Wacquant gestures in point 3:

> [W]elfare "reform" was a forceful intervention into the economy, and one may argue that it has worked to the degree that it has (1) reshaped the dispositions of recipients through intensive "moral rearmament," implying a concurrent and mutually reinforcing degradation of the recipient self and glorification of the working self; (2) transmogrified the categories of perception through which welfare and work are perceived and evaluated so as to (re)sacralize labor and elevate it to the rank of absolute civic duty—as in the slogan, posted on the walls of countless welfare offices, "All Jobs Are Good Jobs"; and (3) pressed the poor into the substandard slots of the unskilled labor market, thereby increasing the supply of pliable workers, accelerating the churning at the bottom of the employment pool, and intensifying the desocialization of wage work, in keeping with the core mission of the "workfare state" all over the capitalist world.[37]

These observations would be at home in the discussion of neoliberalism previously in this chapter. What is different about Wacquant's take are his points 1 and 2: the double transformation of self-evaluation and work-evaluation. Both have an ethical component—neither transformation happens in a vacuum where the recipient merely hears about the changes to the law. It must be communicated and applied through some means. Wacquant often dances around this fact by giving agency to laws and economic systems instead of the bureaucrats who apply the law to the recipients. When Wacquant does deal with the bureaucratic elements, they lack the full-bodied approach of Weber.

[T]he workfare revolution is a *specifically political project* aimed at remaking not only the market but also, and above all, the state itself. The effect of PRWORA in this regard is to recalibrate public authority at three levels: its internal organization (bureaucratic segmentation and differentiation through devolution), its external boundary (redrawing the division of labor between the public and private sectors), and its functional loading (via the penalization of welfare and the shift from the assistantial to the penal treatment of the more disruptive correlates of poverty).[38]

This lack of specificity makes it difficult to pin down Wacquant's conception of bureaucracy. At times, the bureaucracy has retreated before the march of neoliberalism. In others, it has transported from the public to the private sector (usually in the form of dumping off public social services into private for-profit hands). At still other times, the bureaucracy functions as an example of the individual-state power relationship. It may be the case that all three of his characterizations are simultaneously true. Poverty, as both a state of being and a conceptual category, highlights the ways in which the neoliberal, bureaucratic structure fails. Neoliberalism is not the disappearance of the State but its new evolution.

> Effacing the polarizing class structure and the multisided role of the state in molding marginality, they [the public and legislative debates] have powerfully reasserted the fiction according to which poverty is a matter of individual deed and will, and that it would suffice to stoke the matrimonial fire and zeal for work of those on assistance by means of material constraint and moral suasion to defeat the culpable "dependency" they evince. The new law has made this fiction more plausible than ever before by replacing a categorical entitlement with *an individual contract between recipient and state*, and by redefining the core assignment and reorganizing the day-to-day activities of the line staff of welfare offices accordingly—as illustrated by the frequent renaming of welfare administrations as the "Department of Family Independence" and their local agencies as "Job Centers."[39]

Though these job centers may be run by the government bureaucracy, they require openings in the workforce to be effective. The bureaucrat can assist, train, and provide resources, but ultimately is not responsible for the outcome of the welfare recipient. As long as the rules are followed, the bureaucrat's hands remain clean, even if the recipient is unable to achieve success at the end of the process. Process, not outcome, is the true measure of the bureaucrat's skill.

An issue that I do not believe Wacquant takes seriously enough is that of privacy. This is likely due to the big-picture approach that he takes in regards to the data; privacy is an individualized concern. Igo states the questions at the heart of privacy discussions in modern America:

> How much should a society be able to glean about the lives of its own members, and how much of oneself should one willingly reveal? What aspects of a person were worth knowing—and to whom—and which parts were truly one's own? Where and when could an individual's privacy be guaranteed? . . . Were private spaces and thoughts, undiscovered by others, even possible under the conditions of modern life? What would an ever more knowing society mean for the people caught in its net—and for the individual liberties that Americans supposedly prized? To wit: Could known citizens be happy? Were they, in fact, free?[40]

Both Weber and Foucault raise strong reasons for believing the negative to the final questions. Yet the subjective nature of the questions requires the citizen to *know* she is known, that is, to have the awareness that her life is affected, in some way, by the iron bars or stone walls of modern life. Being seen is different from knowing one is being watched. Ignorance is bliss, but is ignorance possible in a knowing and known world?

Of course not. Even those most committed to avoiding the all-seeing eye of the State must know the rules by which the State operates. In America, this is the Sovereign Citizens movement, an eclectic combination of nationalist ideologies, anti-taxation, and conspiracy theories.[41] One thing that all Sovereign Citizens have in common is their lack (or attempted lack) of a paper/digital trail in government records. Fake license plates, driver's licenses, and in extreme cases, lack of birth certificates are ways to hide from the State. No matter how absurd their historical and legal accounts are, Sovereign Citizens have touched a key issue: without the bureaucracy (in the form of data collection) the State has a more difficult time enforcing its will.

Yet, as Igo and others point out, such privacy is an inherent part of the American experiment and other parts of the Western political tradition. The seeds of late nineteenth- and twentieth-century privacy concerns are rooted in the Bill of Rights. The Third, Fourth, and Fifth Amendments all connect to issues of privacy. The Third Amendment is a combination of property and privacy rights as most pre-Civil War issues of privacy were negotiated through property concerns based on Lockean principles. The Fourth Amendment is perhaps the most obvious in relation to modern privacy concerns:

> The right of the people to be secure in their persons, houses, papers, and effects, against unreasonable searches and seizures, shall not be violated, and no Warrants shall issue, but upon probable cause, supported by Oath or affirmation, and particularly describing the place to be searched, and the persons or things to be seized.

The prohibition on unreasonable searches and seizures is explained by detailing the elements necessary for a reasonable search and seizure. There is a privacy right built-in against government intrusion. The Fifth Amendment is likely to be the most controversial of my claims to privacy, but it seems that there is an embryonic right to mental privacy, that I need not expose my guilt to the State. Needless to say, the late eighteenth century did not have the magnitude of bureaucratic power which citizens now face.

Privacy, for the most part, does not exist in the post-conviction judicial system.[42] While certain aspects of privacy are violated before conviction, mostly privacy of the body in regard to others' safety in the form of pat-downs at the time of arrest and more thorough searches before being released into the general prison population, privacy collapses to only attorney-client privilege, and even that occasionally, though unlawfully, breaks down.[43] During my analysis of the judicial system, I will purposefully avoid discussing the merits of the punitive or rehabilitative debate regarding the purpose of prisons. Such discussions are better left to others in sociology and criminology. The tension in Christian ethics favors the rehabilitative, but those traditions which have a greater emphasis on the doctrine of sin find a purpose for punitive systems. My larger concern is the representation of the prison as the collective endgame of the coercive power of the bureaucratic state. The prison is both the negative consequence (see my definition of coercion in chapter 3) and the threat of the negative consequence. That is, the prison symbolizes the power of the State through the example of others to the general public.

The American prison system has many examples to choose from. Just over 1.2 million individuals were imprisoned in 2022—a 20 percent drop over the decade, but a 2 percent increase from 2021.[44] These are simultaneously the most private and exposed individuals in the country. They are private in that they are separated from the general public behind walls, gates, fences, and guards. At the same time, they have no meaningful privacy within the very walls that keep them out of the public eye. This latter concept is best expressed through the Foucauldian "Panopticon." The physical panopticon was meant to be a central hub in an area of surveillance from which those in power could oversee the drill yard or prison hall. The intellectual concept operating in the background is quite simple: the omnipresent coercive threat (bordering on omnipotence as far as its targets were concerned) coupled with omnipresent surveillance (bordering on omniscience) leads to proper behavior (discipline). The metaphorical panopticon takes the intellectual concept and makes one subtle shift: a not-quite omnipresent, omnipotent, omniscient viewer. This "not-quite" concept is important for two reasons: first, the "correct" implementation of the practices which lead to these "omnis" is self-fulfilling. Take the phenomenon of secret police organizations in totalitarian states. If I believe I am being watched by the government, I must discipline myself to not get caught up in some subversive activity. Part of this discipline is watching others and staying clear of those who may be subversive. This can also take the form of informing the secret police of those who do participate in subversive activities (as I believe the police are watching the subversives as well), and a "make sure you note down that *I* reported it" attitude. Through my own fear of State power, I have become a conduit for that power.[45] The second concept is that of freedom. Because of the prisons' expression of State power, freedom is constructed as "not in prison" (e.g., he was *freed* from jail). Another form of self-fulfillment takes place in the citizenry. Freedom is constrained to "not-being-punished." Free speech is that speech for which I cannot be punished; freedom of religion is those practices I participate in and not be punished; and so on. Freedom as not-punishment does not destroy the concept of freedom, but the problem of the binary comes into play. When structured as a binary, freedom or punishment, the full implications of "freedom" are displaced by a state of being in which the State still looms as the negative.

Punishment, in the form of the penal system, goes far beyond surveillance. But even here, the hallmarks of bureaucratic thinking are evident.

> And because the police, the courts, and the prison are, upon close examination, the somber and stern face that the Leviathan turns everywhere toward the dispossessed and dishonored categories trapped in the hollows of the inferior regions of social and urban space by economic deregulation and the retrenchment of schemes of social protection.[46]

Beyond the metaphorical position of the prison, there is one aspect of the American judicial system that needs special attention as it is another expression of the bureaucratic mindset hiding in plain sight. I am referring to the policy of mandatory minimums in sentencing, especially as it relates to illicit drug possession. In this case, it is not the bureaucracy per se that has created the problems. Instead, the problem lies with Congress, which, in passing these laws, has adopted the same mindset as an ideal-type bureaucrat, even from a position of political power. The important point here is that such a mindset has become politically expedient, suggesting how far it has moved beyond its original boundaries (recall in Weber's "Politics as a Vocation" and parts of *Economy and Society* that he draws a sharp distinction between the politician and the bureaucrat). Wacquant notes the greater political reliance upon rules and guidelines for the judiciary:

> Driven by concerns that broad discretion had led to rootless sentencing, unjustifiable in its leniency in some instances and in its severity in others,

legislative bodies moved to curtail discretionary sentencing on several fronts. Determinate sentencing, sentencing commissions and guidelines, and mandatory minimum sentences became more prevalent. Parole and probation were abolished or greatly restricted in several jurisdictions.[47]

The key aspect of mandatory minimums is the removal of discretion in sentencing for certain types of crimes, primarily drug trafficking but also violent crimes and sex crimes. The traditional independence of the judicial system from the worst aspects of politicization is undone when politicians are deciding the sentences and preventing judges from delivering justice in the sense of giving each one their due. Judges are removed from one of the most important aspects of their role in the sentencing process. By setting *rules* in place of discretion, which could be affected by emotion or mitigating circumstances, the criminal justice system is made uniform, adding to the *efficiency* of the system. This efficient uniformity should, in theory, be color-blind, lacking distinctions in class, and speed up the overall process. Instead, in the case of mandatory minimums, racial and class distinctions were indirectly inserted into the law. In the early 2000s, to receive the same mandatory sentence would require one hundred times more powder cocaine than crack cocaine:

> Because of its relative low cost, crack cocaine is more accessible for poor Americans, many of whom are African Americans. Conversely, powder cocaine is much more expensive and tends to be used by more affluent white Americans. Nationwide statistics compiled by the Sentencing Commission reveal that African Americans are more likely to be convicted of crack cocaine offenses, while whites are more likely to be convicted of powder cocaine offenses. Thus, the sentencing disparities punishing crack cocaine offenses more harshly than powder cocaine offenses unjustly and disproportionately penalize African American defendants for drug trafficking comparable to that of white defendants. Compounding the problem is the fact that whites are disproportionately less likely to be prosecuted for drug offenses in the first place; when prosecuted, are more likely to be acquitted; and even if convicted, are much less likely to be sent to prison. Recent data indicates that African Americans make up 15% of the country's drug users, yet they comprise 37% of those arrested for drug violations, 59% of those convicted, and 74% of those sentenced to prison for a drug offense. Specifically with regard to crack, more than 80% of the defendants sentenced for crack offenses are African American, despite the fact that more than 66% of crack users are white or Hispanic.[48]

Ironically, part of the impetus behind mandatory minimums was a concern over disparate sentences for different races.

Foucault's metaphorical Panopticon has also been linked to "the new normal" of heightened surveillance in the post-9/11, 7/7, and Paris attacks world. Before 9/11, prevention as a policing tactic was understood as a show of force, the embodiment of the coercive power of the State, expressed more through the threat of force than force itself. This paradigm was irrevocably altered by the events of 9/11. Coercion is meaningless when the perpetrator is not only willing to die for a cause but uses death as the means to achieve the goal. No level of coercion can deter martyrdom. Thus, prevention shifted from "show-of-force" to "know-beforehand." This necessarily led to the expansion of the surveillance state, most notably in the United States, Great Britain, and France. However, Foucault's Panopticon is more nuanced than mere surveillance. He claims:

> Discipline "makes" individuals; it is the specific technique of a power that regards individuals both as objects and as instruments of its exercise. It is not a triumphant power, which because of its own excess can pride itself on its omnipotence; it is a modest, suspicious power, which functions as a calculated, but permanent economy.[49]

Discipline is the most subtle technique of power that the bureaucratic system uses.

> The exercise of discipline presupposes a mechanism that coerces by means of observation; an apparatus in which the techniques that make it possible to see induce effects of power, and in which conversely, the means of coercion make those on whom they are applied clearly visible.[50]

I will return to the idea of "being seen" momentarily. After a discussion of the minutiae of an army camp, Foucault explains,

> A whole problematic then develops: that of an architecture that is no longer built simply to be seen (as with the ostentation of palaces), or to observe the external space (cf. the geometry of fortresses), but to permit an internal, articulated and detailed control—architecture that would operate to transform individuals: to act on those it shelters, to provide a hold on their conduct, to carry the effects of power right to them, to make it possible to know them, to alter them. Stones can make people docile and knowable.[51]

So can iron cages. Weber's metaphor for modernity is strikingly similar to Foucault's concept of discipline. Foucault's five infinitive forms are five attempts at saying the same thing. To know is to have power and to know someone is to have power over that person.[52] But how does such knowing-power manifest? Though he does not name it as such, Foucault is clearly describing specialized bureaucrats in specific fields: the "clerks, supervisors and foremen"[53] of manufacturing or the advanced students and assistant teachers who were part pedagogue, part surveyor of the behavior of the classroom.⁵⁴ Both groups not only engaged in surveillance but in recording their surveillance. The records can be passed up the hierarchy, allowing the superiors to act. We once again see the dynamic of the data collector and the data analyst. The bureaucrat is nothing without data. However, it is not always negative data. "Surveillance" has taken on a connotation of negativity, either in the material/persons being watched or in the motivations of the watchers. In the previous two examples, a foreman may discover an overly productive worker who could be tasked with more difficult jobs, or the assistant teacher may realize that a child's behavior issues come from the boredom of having mastered the material and needing to progress onward.

Such "surveillance" is not bad, but does it transgress some ethical lines we would not like to cross? Aspects of the Western legal-judicial system have built-in moral assumptions, especially the importance of protecting the innocent. Blackstone's famous ratio, "Better that ten guilty persons escape, than that one innocent suffer," is at the heart of the Common Law tradition.⁵⁵ In a piece replete with sarcasm,⁵⁶ Volokh makes some interesting points regarding religious values lying behind Blackstone's and others' ratios of guilty (expressed as the variable $n$) to innocent:

> Abraham's celebrated haggle in the book of Genesis, allegedly written by Moses but also attributed to God, provisionally sets a value of n at (P-10)/10, where P is the population of Sodom. As it turns out, however, no innocents were killed in the destruction of Sodom: There were only four righteous people in the city, and they were all saved, although they lost their real estate. Previously, God had killed the entire human population of the Earth because of its wickedness (except for Noah and his family) in a mass capital punishment which, although carried out without the benefits of a jury or any other due process protections, apparently also produced neither false positives nor false negatives. It is said that one day there will be another massive (post-) capital punishment, which will also produce neither false positives nor false negatives. These methods, however, may only be acceptable criminal procedure for God Himself, Who may do whatever He likes.
>
> Commandments to man can be found in the book of Exodus, by the same Author(s), in which God rejects the tradeoff between convicting the guilty and convicting the innocent, and simply commands, "the innocent and righteous slay thou not."
>
> Not all gods, however, agree with the Exalted One. The Roman emperor Trajan, who was later deified, wrote to Adsidius Severus that a person ought not "to be condemned on suspicion; for it was preferable that the crime of a guilty man should go unpunished than an innocent man be condemned." For the Romans, then, n = 1 for all cases where a man is to be "condemned," which includes capital cases.

94                                        *Chapter 4*

   The most celebrated divine commandment related to punishing the innocent is, of course, Blackstone's. Evidence of Blackstone's divinity is provided by an Arkansas district court, which ruled in 1991 that "Blackstone is, in the law at least, immortal," and evidence of His miraculous works is supplied by Lord Avonmore, who wrote: "He it was that first gave the law the air of science. He found it a skeleton, and clothed it with life, color and complexion; he embraced the cold statute, and by his touch it grew into youth, health, and beauty." Blackstone's $n = 10$ applies in all cases of suffering, which is a broader category than both Yahweh's and Trajan's.[57]

The legal system, given the possibility for ultimate outcomes (namely in capital punishment, but extending to the negative effects of a felony conviction on one's record), necessarily builds in safeguards against overreach and mistakes. Even with these safeguards, mistakes can be made. I contend that bureaucratic systems have no similar built-in morality and lack the safeguards that bureaucratic systems claim to have. We are forced to return to MacIntyre's (mis)reading of Weber to fully investigate this claim. Recall that efficiency is the highest good for the bureaucrat and increasingly for those invested in the neoliberal order. Finishing the interaction between the bureaucrat and the civilian correctly, according to the bureaucratic rules established, is more important than fairness or justice in the particular situation. Hopefully, the bureaucratic rules are written in such a way that fairness, justice, and other virtuous outcomes are possible, though we have seen that this is not always the case. If the outcome is negative for the civilian, however, it is not the fault of the bureaucrat given that she followed the proper procedures. The innocent may suffer due to the procedural "rules" of the bureaucracy while the guilty may be able to work the procedures to their own advantages. Yet, the misapplication of justice does not have to be a byproduct of corruption. Injustice takes on an overly moral hue from the developments of Christian thinking. The prophetic tradition in the Old Testament is primarily concerned with justice. More than half the occurrences of the Hebrew *mišpāṭ*, the predominant word used for justice in the Old Testament, are in the prophetic literature. Justice requires a vigilant disposition as it is cultivated (grown, tended to) and not the norm of society. The effect of sin is too strong on humanity for societies to "reset" to justice. In fact, the tradition claims that sin has affected all areas of life to some degree. This allows for the concept of structural inequality. Occasionally in religious contexts, the phrase structural sin will be used instead of inequality. I argue that the intention behind the phrase "structural sin" is well-meaning but ultimately misguided unless several nuances are made clear. First, the "sins" of which the structures participate in are not the fault of those currently working within the structure. Such sins were committed by powerful people who were able to integrate their misguided views into a bureaucratic or another institutional system. Another important and under-developed concept is how sin affects the sinner. It is not only the victims of sin who are affected but the ones who carry them out as well. Finally, the forgiveness of sin for the individual does not nullify the negative effects of sin in the world to which that individual already contributed. History provides many examples. The US allowance for slavery, even by the same men who signed the Declaration of Independence and helped form the Constitution, is both the peculiar institution and the first sin.[58] The guilt of slavery is in the past, but the effects of slavery as a sin continue today. The guilt of Jim Crow laws is (mainly) in the past, but the effects of these sinful practices still continue today. Any guilt or sin on these issues today is the result of willful ignorance as to the negative effects of the past. Thus, to say that the United States suffers from the structural sin of racism is to say that sometime in the past, those who could have acted differently did not, and allowed a sin of horrific magnitude to be institutionalized into the fabric of society. Removing such sinful effects from the fabric leaves a hole, the after-effects of sins. Sewing a patch in place may diminish those effects, but we cannot undo sin. Thus, even if a society were to escape the bureaucratization of bodies, it will still have to deal with the lingering damage caused.

Before concluding this section, I want to turn to a fictional literary character who may help to explain the double bureaucratization I have laid out in this chapter. This figure is Dickens's classic figure of Ebenezer Scrooge. The character is so classic that the name Scrooge has become synonymous with miserliness and a pitiless attitude. His early depiction is one of a man who cares only for the bottom line.[59] His obsession leads to his breakup and his literally cold attitude toward his employees and others.[60] But the connection between Scrooge's hyper-capitalist mindset and the bureaucratization of bodies occurs before the arrival of the Ghosts. The unnamed charity collectors who visit Scrooge's office bear the brunt of his views on the plight of the poor.

*Charity Collector:* Now then sir, about the donation?
*Scrooge:* Well now, let's see. I know how to treat the poor. My taxes go to pay for the prisons and the poorhouses. The homeless must go there.
*Charity Collector:* But some would rather die.
*Scrooge:* If they'd rather die, then they'd better do it . . . and decrease the surplus population![61]

Scrooge's statement sounds like those whom Wacquant and others in the prison reform movement criticize today. Of course, Scrooge's story does not end there. Is there a similar "redemption" to be found against the more oppressive and more controlling systems of our contemporary bureaucratic world?

## BUREAUCRATIZATION OF KNOWLEDGE

Lastly, we turn to the most technocratic of the examples: public health. This is a major shift from the previous two chapters where the bureaucracy was acting upon individuals in vulnerable situations. There, the discussion centered on the uncommon, but not unusual, circumstances a large but by no means a majority, number of individuals experienced. Here, the concern is on a unique situation, with worldwide ramifications. The COVID-19 pandemic could certainly qualify as a Schmittian exception. It should come as no surprise, given the previous explorations of bureaucratic systems and neoliberalism, that the power vacuum of this exception was filled by an alliance of the two.

This chapter has three parts. First, an analysis of public health as an ethical discourse. Second, an analysis of public health as a field of bureaucratic control and the attendant coercion which differs from the examples in the previous chapter. Third, a critique of the major bureaucratic response to the COVID-19 pandemic, censorship. This final part illustrates the dangers when bureaucratic regimes move too far away from their ideal-type neutrality.

As the COVID-19 response is still politically charged and may color our perspectives, I want to make some general comments at the beginning. My analysis of individuals and institutions, their decisions, actions, or comments should be understood through the larger critique of bureaucratic regimes and mindsets. The decisions of elected officials have little bearing on the following discussions, save when those decisions are clearly made at the urging of bureaucratic officials. Even though these events are in the not-too-distant past, we must be aware of making judgments in hindsight. Moral judgments can only be made after the historical record is constructed.

## PUBLIC HEALTH AS AN ETHICAL DISCOURSE

Public health campaigns, initiatives, and mandates are the most likely points of contact between the bureaucratic state and the average citizen in our examples. Before moving on to the bureaucratic aspects, we must first trace the contours of public health as a discourse.

Like other major government or government-adjacent institutions and systems, public health campaigns require the buy-in of the public. "Public trust and confidence are essential in public health emergency preparedness and response, and public health decision-making will be most effective generally when it is transparent and has direct links to the communities it serves."[62]

What falls under the category of public health problems and why is such a label compelling? I turn to the latter first. Verweij and Dawson list five possibilities: an epidemiological issue ("common or increasing in the population"), a causation issue ("influenced to some extent by socio-economic and other background conditions"), a responsibility issue ("collective or governmental rather than individual action"), a polity issue ("threaten important values in society and that this justifies particular forms of intervention"), and a normative issue ("particular emphasis or urgency . . . stopping them as an important moral issue"). They also note that "There is no reason to think that these explanations are mutually exclusive" as all five could apply to many of the public health crises in the past half-century.[63] Of these issues, only the first (epidemiological) seems to lack interaction with the type of bureaucratic systems on which I am focusing. The final issue, that of normativity, seems to be a necessary component of any justifiable coercive governmental action. On the problem of normativity, Jennings notes,

> In truth, the requirements of normative justification are quite demanding in the arena of public health because changes of the magnitude required usually involve some form of state action—the creation of legal sanctions and enforcement, the creation of administrative structures, the investment and allocation of resources, and the mobilization of popular support.[64]

Without using the same terminology, Jennings is describing the bureaucratic regime I have sketched in the previous chapters: coercion, bodies/knowledge, and a market-like system to deploy and encourage the changes in question. Beyond normativity, the combination of responsibility and polity components is also critical to this study. When a situation meets these two conditions, governmental action is justified due to the collective threat to some collective good.

Given that COVID-19 was respiratory and quite contagious, the epidemiological and responsibility conditions are met.[65] Some of the comorbidities with COVID-19 were connected to socio-economic or other environmental factors, appearing to satisfy the causation condition. The normative condition was satisfied by the early death rate, in which COVID-19 raced through elderly populations and those with respiratory comorbidities. The extrapolation of these early data points led to the polity condition—due to the expected numbers of cases and deaths, hospitals will be overrun, medical supplies will become scarce, and the health care system writ large will be pushed to the limits—thus, to protect the social good of their respective health systems, governments must intervene in extreme ways, leading to the "two weeks to stop the spread" lockdown justification.

Ethical considerations cannot be "armchair" or "Monday morning" quarterbacking. As such, the behavior of both governmental and private organizations through the fall of 2020 can only be criticized on what was known at the time. October 4, 2020, is the first public pivot point in the narrative with the release of "The Great Barrington Declaration" (GBD), an open letter written by three public health experts and signed by many others, who advocated that governments should "allow those who are at minimal risk of death to live their lives normally to build up immunity to the virus through natural infection, while better protecting those who are at highest risk."[66] This letter was published before the vaccine rollout and a month before the 2020 elections in the United States. The response within the official public health apparatus was to dismiss and attempt to undermine the policy arguments made in the GBD.[67]

As of this writing, we are approaching the four-year anniversary of the first lockdowns. History, like our understanding of COVID-19, has progressed. We now know that the response to the pandemic was just as often a bureaucratic decision as it was a scientific decision. The central claim of this chapter is that governmental bureaucratic officials in the public health field attempted to fill the sovereignty void. In doing so, these officials blurred the lines between technocratic experts and sovereign decision-makers. Recent polling suggests that the ill-effects of this process are already here.[68]

According to the best timeline available, the problem of bureaucrats and COVID-19 began in January 2020—two to three months before the lockdowns began in the United States.

The censorship-coercion nexus is best expressed through the Preliminary Motion ruling in *Missouri v. Biden* (which on appeal was renamed *Murthy v. Missouri*) by Judge Terry A. Doughty. As of this writing, the Supreme Court has stayed the injunction but has not yet heard oral arguments. At the preliminary stage of a civil case, all evidence must be read in the light most favorable to the plaintiff, thus Judge Doughty stated, "If the allegations made by Plaintiffs are true, the present case arguably involves the most massive attack against free speech in United States' history."[69] The complaint lists nine total areas of censorship, but the three which focus on COVID-19 are "(2) suppressing speech about the lab-leak theory of COVID-19's origin; (3) suppressing speech about the efficiency of masks and COVID-19 lockdowns; (4) suppressing speech about the efficiency of COVID-19 vaccines."[70]

At an objective level, the key problem is that the lab-leak theory is now supported by the US Department of Energy and the FBI, but not supported by other executive-branch departments.[71] The National Intelligence Council's declassified report on COVID-19 suggests seven different US intelligence programs investigated the origins and came to a 4-1-3 split: four in favor of natural development, one in favor of the lab-leak theory (likely in reference to the FBI's intelligence operations), and three unable to come to a consensus based on the data available.[72] This is the major problem with the bureaucrat-as-expert construction. The bureaucrat is still human, still capable of making mistakes, especially in the field of science. Again, the problem is not that the science itself changed but that the authoritative nature of the declaration changes. According to the censorship regime in the early days of the pandemic, the Department of Energy and the FBI would be guilty of disinformation or misinformation. We must briefly turn to the distinction between these two terms before unpacking the censorship arguments.

The accepted framework of disinformation is that it is factually wrong and is, therefore, not information at all. Misinformation is factually correct but is missing context in some way. According to Sille Obelitz Søe, the problem with dis- and misinformation conceptions is the built-in notion of truth and falsity.[73] Instead, Søe argues that we should understand intentionality and "misleadingness" as the double axis. Thus, *information* (which seems to equate to factually true statements) carries the intention of being non-misleading, *disinformation* (which seems to equate to factually false statements) carries the intention of being misleading, and misinformation does not carry the intention of being misleading. As Søe notes, this approach allows other forms of speech rather than purely declarative statements to pass the test—"Irony, for instance, can be literally false but still be intentionally non-misleading information—in exactly the same way as misinformation and disinformation can be literally true but still be misleading, either unintendedly or intentionally."[74]

The problem with Søe's model is the difficulty in ascertaining another's intentionality. This problem is multiplied given the impersonal nature of most social media. The lack of a sarcasm font makes social media communication that much more complicated. The intentionality behind a joke or satire is even more difficult to distinguish. The bureaucrats involved in the censorship attempts in question did not refer to the intention of the speech they censored. However, they did seem to develop a system in which their own intentions justified their actions with the creation of *malinformation*. Malinformation is true and not misleading factual statements that undermine some goal of the decision-makers on the censorship front and thus should be repressed. Factually true statements about vaccine side-effects in general—even when such generality was specified—could be malinformation if the censors believed it could cause COVID-19 vaccine hesitancy among the population.[75]

One of the major counter-arguments to the First Amendment violations claimed by the petitioners is that the social media companies are private and therefore free to police speech in ways the US government is unable.[76] These companies have their own respective terms of service (TOS) which users must abide by and (as private companies) do not have to collect feedback from users when considering changes to the respective TOS agreements. While there have been some counters to these claims,[77] they are less important than the argument made by the plaintiffs that coercive pressure placed on these companies by governmental officials, many of them the quintessential definition of bureaucrats and technocrats, transformed private social media companies into state agents. "Traditionally, the First Amendment imposes limitations only on 'state action, not action by private parties.' . . . However, plaintiffs 'may establish a First Amendment claim based on private conduct if that conduct 'can fairly be seen as state action.'"[78]

Judge Doughty continues,

> Government action can exist in at least five circumstances: (1) action that results from the State's exercise of "coercive power," . . . (2) action that results from the state providing "significant encouragement, either overt or covert," to a private action, . . . (3) action that results from a private actor operating as a willful participant in joint activity with the State or its agents, . . . (4) action that is entwined with governmental policies, or when the government is entwined in the management or control of the private action, . . . and (5) action with specific features that combines to create a compelling case for state action, especially where a federal statute has immunized private conduct.[79]

President Biden seems to have threatened Facebook when, in admittedly off-the-cuff remarks to reporters before leaving the White House, the following exchange took place:

*Reporter:* "On COVID misinformation, what's your message to platforms like Facebook?"
*Biden:* "They're killing people, I mean it—look, the only pandemic we have is among the unvaccinated and that they're killing people."[80]

Contextually, it is clear that Biden meant "platforms like Facebook," to which Facebook responded with a spokesperson saying, "We will not be distracted by accusations which aren't supported by the facts."[81] However, in a townhall with CNN a few days later, Biden claimed,

> [Y]ou may have heard—I never get myself in trouble, as you know, politically—(laughs)—but you may have heard that I was critical of some of the things that are on Facebook, and it was that I was attacking Facebook. I wasn't attacking

Facebook. There was a report out saying that for that—something like 45 percent of the overwhelming disinformation on Facebook comes from 12 individuals. I said: They're killing people—those 12 individuals; that misinformation is going to kill people. Not a joke. Not a joke.[82]

Even if we accept Biden's statement as true and not political spin (which is belied by the fact that the "killing" comment does not appear on the official White House transcript site), the fact that Facebook believed it was being targeted moves the statement very close to coercive in nature.

Yet, as I pointed to in earlier chapters, the sovereign (or in this case, symbolic sovereign) does not need to do the threating for it to be coercive. The nature of the coercion is best illustrated through the documents made public (in slightly redacted form) for the *Missouri v. Biden* case. Some of the key emails come from Rob Flaherty, who was then Director of Digital Strategy for the Biden White House, and Andy Slavitt, who was then the senior advisor for COVID response. The clearest threat comes from a March 15, 2021, email from Slavitt:

> I do feel like relative to others, interactions with Facebook are not straightforward and the problems are worse—like you are trying to meet a minimum hurdle instead of trying to solve the problem and we have to ask you precise questions and even then we get highly scrubbed party line answers. We have urgency and don't sense it from you all. 100% of the questions I asked have never been answered and weeks have gone by. Internally we have been considering our options on what to do about it.[83]

The final line is difficult to interpret in any way other than a threat, as internally means, at minimum, the West Wing, if not the Oval Office itself. In April, Flaherty twice mentions the events of January 6, 2021.

> Will say I'm really mostly interested in what effects the interventions and products you've tested have had on increasing vaccine interest within hesitant communities, and which ones have shown promise. Really couldn't care less about products unless they're having measurable impact. And while the product safari has been interesting, at the end of the day, I care mostly about what actions and changes you're making to ensure sure you're not making our country's vaccine hesitancy problem worse. I definitely have what I believe to be a non-comprehensive list of products you're building but I still don't have a good, empirical answer on how effective you've been at reducing the spread of vaccine-skeptical content and misinformation to vaccine fence sitters in the now-folded "lockdown." If [redacted] can speak to those things, great. [redacted] hasn't been able to, but I'm sure someone there can.
>
> In the electoral context, you tested and deployed an algorithmic shift that promoted quality news and information about the election. This was reported

in the New York Times and also readily apparent to anyone with cursory social listening tools. You only did this, however, after an election that you helped increase skepticism in, and an insurrection which was plotted, in large part, on your platform. And then you turned it back off. I want some assurances, based in data, that you are not doing the same thing again here.[84]

In an email from April 14, 2021, Flaherty ends an email critical of Facebook's decision to not remove a Tucker Carlson video (and only demote it) with the line "Not for nothing but last time we did this dance, it ended in an insurrection."[85] Flaherty's first email listed here implies Facebook's responsibility for the events of January 6—even though Section 270 of the Communications Act makes it clear Facebook cannot be liable for third-party usage of the platform. The April 14 email is more nuanced in isolation—January 6 was possible because people like Carlson were able to spread dis- or misinformation. Taken together, these two emails have something of an edge to them. Most importantly, however, is to take all three emails in the wider political context of Section 270. On March 25, 2021, a (virtual) hearing before the Subcommittee on Communications and Technology and the Subcommittee on Consumer Protection and Commerce of the Committee on Energy and Commerce of the House was held, entitled "Disinformation Nation: Social Media's Role in Promoting Extremism and Misinformation." The witnesses were Mark Zuckerberg of Facebook (now Meta), Sundar Pichai of Alphabet (Google and YouTube's parent company), and Jack Dorsey, former CEO of Twitter (now X). The opening statement of Mike Doyle lays the blame for January 6 and vaccine hesitancy at the feet of these three companies. He ends by saying,

> Your companies need to be held accountable. We need rules, regulations, technical experts in government, and audit authority of your technologies. Ours is the committee of jurisdiction, and we will legislate to stop this. The stakes are simply too high.[86] This statement is not coercive, but it is what gives Flaterhy's emails a few weeks later their threatening undertone. There was bipartisan support for ending Section 230 protections, which seemed to fade after each company worked more closely with the Biden administration.[87]

## CONCLUSION

These case studies show the multifaceted power of coercive bureaucracies, even in situations where the bureaucratic structure is meant to be supportive of individuals. The vast majority of social workers and scientists want to help people, not harm them. Unfortunately, the nature of bureaucratic thinking (exacerbated by neoliberal views of humanity) creates situations in which harm is inevitable and help is less than likely. These case studies also highlight the range of power bureaucratic systems have. The power dynamic between the welfare recipient and the welfare bureaucrat is similar to that of social media users and those capable of coercing social media companies. The effects may be different—it would be difficult to claim that the dehumanization Wacquant points to is the same as having a social media post unfairly deleted—but the bureaucratic mindset is still functioning.

## NOTES

1. William Mitchell and Thomas Fazi, *Reclaiming the State: A Progressive Vision of Sovereignty for a Post-Neoliberal World* (London: Pluto Press, 2017), 1-2; Aaron Major, *Architects of Austerity: International Finance and the Politics of Growth* (Stanford, CA: Stanford University Press, 2014), 189–190.

2. Colin Hay, *Why We Hate Politics* (Cambridge, MA: Polity Press, 2007), 97.

3. Mitchell and Fazi note that Joan Robinson was the first to use "bastard Keynesianism," 28.

4. Mitchell and Fazi, 33.

5. On the details and possible interpretations, see Mitchell and Fazi, 33–35 and 43–45; Rawi Abdelal, *Capital Rules: The Construction of Global Finance* (Cambridge, MA: Harvard University Press, 2009), 34–35; Major, 193–194.

6. Quinn Slobodian, *Globalists: The End of Empire and the Birth of Neoliberalism* (Cambridge, MA: Harvard University Press, 2018), 30ff.

7. Right-wing criticisms of neoliberalism are often centered on a particular aspect of neoliberalism (such as the effect of globalization on the disruption of communities that were previously supported by manufacturing) and not the system as a whole. Part of the difference between left and right critiques is the general affinity of right-wing thinkers to the concept of the "free market." This can range from the libertarian position (which is adjacent to ideal-type neoliberalism) to more centrist positions that presume the free market while allowing for government intervention in those areas where the market is unequipped or unable to function properly (public utilities and infrastructure, for example, or Keynesianism-lite interventions).

8. Deborah Johnston and Alfredo Saad-Filho, *Neoliberalism: A Critical Reader* (London: Pluto Press, 2005), 9. I am unsure if the allusion is intended, but "the beast" brings to mind the beast of Revelation 13, who requires a mark for anyone wishing to buy or sell goods. Contemporary neoliberalism would seem to fit the bill for these authors. It is also interesting that this work was published three years before the Financial Crash.

9. Wendy Brown, *Undoing the Demos: Neoliberalism's Stealth Revolution* (New York: Zone Books, 2015), 9.

10. I am unaware of any serious proposals from a neoliberal perspective to do away with the structures of the State entirely. At the very least, the law and order

operations of the State would have to remain to ensure the safe operation of the neoliberal project.

11. Adam Kotsko, *Neoliberalism's Demons: On the Political Theology of Late Capital* (Stanford, CA: Stanford University Press, 2018).

12. Brown, *Undoing*, 17.

13. See Robert Rothman, *Something in Common: The Common Core Standards and the Next Chapter in American Education* (Cambridge, MA: Harvard Education Press, 2011), 9–35, for a pro-standardization argument. I would also draw attention to his emphasis on efficiency for curriculum designers and the goal of preparing students to be competitive in a global market. These are the buzzwords of both bureaucracies and neoliberalism.

14. Kotsko, 87. This theory may explain the role sports has had in integrating American society along a number of previously marginalized groups. Sports is about wins and losses; anyone who can contribute to more of the former and less of the latter becomes valued. The non-athletic traits which are a part of the athlete (race, gender, sexuality) are more easily accepted because the athlete is on "our team." At present, this does not include the issue of transgender sports participation.

15. Other institutions which appear in quotations in this chapter include the World Trade Organization (WTO), the G7 (Group of Seven made up of the United States, Canada, the UK, France, Germany, Italy, and Japan; had been the G8 including Russia until 2014), the Organisation for Economic Co-operation and Development (OECD), the Bank for International Settlements (BIS).

16. Phyllis Mentzell Ryder, "In(ter)ventions of Global Democracy: An Analysis of the Rhetorics of the A-16 World Bank/IMF Protests in Washington, DC," *Rhetoric Review* 25, no. 4 (October 2006): 413. Emphasis original.

17. Major, 191.

18. Ibid., 192–193.

19. Irina Andone and Beatrice Scheubel, "Once Bitten: New Evidence on the Link between IMF Conditionality and IMF Stigma," *European Central Bank Working Paper Series*, no. 2262 (April 12, 2019), 2–3.

20. John E. Stapleford, *Bulls, Bears and Golden Calves: Applying Christian Ethics in Economics*, 3rd ed. (Downers Grove: IVP Academic, 2015), 243.

21. Ngaire Woods, *The Globalizers: The IMF, the World Bank, and Their Borrowers* (Ithaca, NY: Cornell University Press, 2006), 4.

22. Barry Eichengreen and Ngaire Woods, "The IMF's Unmet Challenges," *Journal of Economic Perspectives* 30, no. 1 (Winter 2015): 42.

23. Stapleford, 244.

24. Pierre Bourdieu, "The Abdication of the State," in *The Weight of the World*, trans. Priscilla Parkhurst Ferguson (Stanford, CA: Stanford University Press, 1999), 183.

25. Ibid.

26. Ibid.

27. Émile Durkheim, *The Elementary Forms of Religious Life*, trans. Carol Cosman (New York: Oxford University Press, 2001); Mary Douglas, *Purity and Danger* (New York: Routledge, 2002).

28. Sarah E. Igo, *The Known Citizen: A History of Privacy in Modern America* (Cambridge, MA: Harvard University Press, 2018). I take slight issue with the adjectival tense "known" which suggests a state of completion. The more cumbersome "knowing-of-persons" retains the active and continual nature of the process.

29. Ibid., 2.

30. This is also apparent in the entomology of "political words." *Republic* is from the Latin *res publica*; literally "public things."

31. Welfare was also racialized in the post-Civil Rights era, but for the sake of simplicity, race will be treated separately below.

32. Wacquant, 101. Emphasis original. Wacquant seems to back off the language of singular agency in regard to the American state, see 108.

33. The final votes in the House and Senate were 328-101 with five not voting and 78-21 with one not voting, respectively. On the House vote, see http://clerk.house.gov/evs/1996/roll383.xml (Accessed March 2, 2020) and for the Senate vote, see https://www.senate.gov/legislative/LIS/roll_call_lists/roll_call_vote_cfm.cfm?congress=104&session=2&vote=00262 (Accessed March 2, 2020).

34. Wacquant, 79.

35. Office of Family Assistance, "Characteristics and Financial Circumstances of TANF Recipients Fiscal Year (FY) 2022," (Department of Health and Human Services, October 30, 2023), Tables 17 and 18.

36. Ibid., Table 22. Eighty-five percent of adult recipients were either never married or divorced.

37. Wacquant, 101–102.

38. Ibid., 103. Emphasis original.

39. Ibid., 100–101. Emphasis mine.

40. Igo, 1–2.

41. J. M. Berger, *Without Prejudice: What Sovereign Citizens Believe* (Washington, DC: George Washington Program on Extremism, June 2016), https://extremism.gwu.edu/sites/g/files/zaxdzs5746/files/downloads/JMB%20Sovereign%20Citizens.pdf.

42. Another area is entry into the Armed Services in the form of "boot camp." I will occasionally draw parallels between the judicial system and boot camp, but the most important point of difference between the two is the voluntary nature (save in times of draft) of the US military. Wacquant uses "boot camp" with a non-military meaning at 173.

43. See *United States v. Carter,* No. 16-20032-02-JAR (Dist. Kan. January 25, 2019), in which a federal judge held an entire prosecutorial office in contempt for violating attorney-client privilege at a local prison.

44. E. Ann Carson and Rich Kluckow, "Prisoners in 2022—Statistical Tables," *Bureau of Justice Statistics*, November 2023, 5.

45. In the context of a military boot camp (and some sports practices), punishments for infractions are suffered by the entire group. This leads to self-policing among the group, not reporting, in order to avoid collective punishments.

46. Wacquant, xviii.

47. Charles Doyle, *Federal Mandatory Minimum Sentencing Statutes* (Washington, DC: Congressional Research Service, September 9, 2013), 6.

48. Deborah J. Vagins and Jesselyn McCurdy, *Cracks in the System: Twenty Years of the Unjust Federal Crack Cocaine Law* (Washington, DC: The American Civil Liberties Union, 2006), i.

49. Foucault, 170.

50. Ibid., 170–171.

51. Ibid., 172.

52. This truism is perhaps best expressed in the fable of Rumpelstiltskin.

53. Foucault, 175.

54. Ibid., 175–176.

55. Alexander Volokh, "N Guilty Men," *University of Pennsylvania Law Review*, no. 1 (1997): 173–216.

56. Volokh's final sentence in the introduction is, "n guilty men, then. The travels and metamorphoses of n through all lands and eras are the stuff that epic miniseries are made of. n is the father of criminal law. This is its story." One can almost hear the famous "dun-dun" from the television series *Law & Order* at the end of the sentence. Ibid.

57. Ibid., 177–179.

58. Of course, even these men were born into a society that was unable to deal with the conflict between the Christian message and the institution of racialized slavery. The conflict was absorbed into religiously motivated abolitionism or religiously motivated defenses of slavery.

59. The character is so well known that multiple films have attempted to portray Scrooge. The version which I believe best communicates the emotion of *A Christmas Carol*, though certainly taking very few steps in maintaining accuracy to the text, is the portrayal by Michael Caine and the Muppets in *The Muppet Christmas Carol*. This is not only due to Caine's stature as an actor (even more so when interacting with the various non-human Muppets), but the additional aspect of the movie as a musical. This heightens the emotional aspect of certain key points (especially the appearance of the Marley Brothers and the breakup with his fiancée). Brian Henson, *The Muppet Christmas Carol* (Walt Disney Pictures, 1992). The song "When Love Is Gone" (the breakup song) was not included in the theatrical release, but did appear in VHS and DVD versions. See Padraig Cotter, "The Muppets Christmas Carol: Why 'When Love Is Gone' Is Missing in Some Cuts," *ScreenRant*, March 2, 2020, https://screenrant.com/muppets-christmas-carol-when-love-gone-cut-reason/ (Accessed March 5, 2020).

60. In the vision with the spirit of Christmas Yet-to-Come, Scrooge's possessions are being sold (possibly after being stolen from his estate) after his death. In the Henson version, there is the following exchange between the buyer and seller: "'Why. Mrs. Dilber. they're still warm. I don't pay extra for the warmth, you know.' 'You should, it's the only warmth he ever had.'" The lack of warmth is also connected to Scrooge's miserly use of coal in his office.

61. Henson. The charity collectors are played by Bunsen and Beaker.

62. Barbara A. Ellis, Drue H. Barrett, John D. Arras, and Bruce Jennings, "Introduction," in *Emergency Ethics: Public Health Preparedness and Response* (New York: Oxford University Press, 2016), xxi.

63. Marcel Verweij and Angus Dawson, "The Meaning of 'Public' in 'Public Health'," in *Ethics, Prevention, and Public Health*, ed. Angus Dawson and Marcel Verweij (New York: Oxford University Press, 2007), 14.

64. Bruce Jennings, "Public Health and Civic Republicanism: Toward an Alternative Framework for Public Health Ethics," in *Ethics, Prevention, and Public Health*, ed. Angus Dawson and Marcel Verweij (New York: Oxford University Press, 2007), 31.

65. This combination differentiates COVID-19 from other significant epidemics such as HIV/AIDS in the 1980s or the Ebola outbreaks of the 1990s and 2000s.

66. Martin Kulldorff, Sunetra Gupta, and Jay Bhattacharya, "The Great Barrington Declaration," October 4, 2020, https://gbdeclaration.org/.

67. Jimmy Tobias, "Unredacted NIH Emails Show Efforts to Rule Out Lab Origin of Covid," *The Intercept*, January 19, 2023, https://theintercept.com/2023/01/19/covid-origin-nih-emails/.

68. Pew Research Center, "Americans' Trust in Scientists, Positive Views of Science Continue to Decline," November 2023.

69. *Missouri v. Biden*, No. 3:22-CV-01213 (U.S. Dist. Ct. W. Dist. La. Monroe Div., July 4, 2023), 2. Thus, as of this writing, it is best to understand any claims of censorship as alleged, but very likely, in terms of legal claims.

70. Ibid., 4.

71. Sheryl Gay Stolberg, Benjamin Mueller, and Carl Zimmer, "The Origins of the Covid Pandemic: What We Know and Don't Know," *New York Times*, March 17, 2023, https://www.nytimes.com/article/covid-origin-lab-leak-china.html. The Department of Energy has low confidence of a lab leak while the FBI has moderate confidence.

72. National Intelligence Council, "Updated Assessment on COVID-19 Origins," Office of the Director of National Intelligence, October 29, 2021, 1, 6–9, https://www.dni.gov/files/ODNI/documents/assessments/Declassified-Assessment-on-COVID-19-Origins.pdf.

73. Sille Obelitz Søe, "A Unified Account of Information, Misinformation, and Disinformation," *Synthese* 198, no. 6 (June 2021): 5929–5949.

74. Ibid., 5947.

75. The anecdotal nature of such claims may admittedly complicate the true/false distinction.

76. "Under this theory, Plaintiffs' claims fail as a matter of law because the First Amendment imposes limitations only on state action, not action by private parties," *Missouri v. Biden*, 55.

77. Most of these arguments revolve around readings of the Communications Act of 1934 (amended by the Telecom Act of 1996), 47 U.S.C. § 230(c)(1) which exempts "providers . . . of an interactive computer service" from being liable for material other parties exchange on the platform, or wider policy arguments—for example, large social media platforms have transformed their platforms into utilities or public spaces, both of which have higher thresholds for speech suppression.

78. *Missouri v. Biden*, 56. Internal citations omitted.

79. Ibid., 56–57. Internal citations omitted.

80. "President Biden White House Departure," C-SPAN, July 16, 2021, https://www.c-span.org/video/?513464-1/president-biden-white-house-departure. There is no official transcript of this encounter on the White House website, even though there are transcripts of similarly short discussions with the press.

81. Zolan Kanno-Youngs and Cecilia Kang, "'They're Killing People': Biden Denounces Social Media for Virus Disinformation," *New York Times*, July 16 (updated July 19), 2021.

82. Joe Biden, "Remarks by President Biden in a CNN Town Hall with Don Lemon," *The White House*, July 22, 2021, https://www.whitehouse.gov/briefing-room/speeches-remarks/2021/07/22/remarks-by-president-biden-in-a-cnn-town-hall-with-don-lemon/.

83. *Missouri v. Biden*, Exhibit A—Document #174, Attachment 1—Email from Andy Slavitt, March 15, 2021.

84. Ibid., Email from Rob Flaherty, April 9, 2021.

85. Ibid., Email from Rob Flaherty, April 14, 2021.

86. "Disinformation Nation: Social Media's Role in Promoting Extremism and Misinformation" (Washington, DC, March 25, 2021), https://www.congress.gov/event/117th-congress/house-event/111407/text.

87. The Supreme Court reversed the *Murthy v. Missouri* case on the grounds that the original plaintiffs lacked Article III due to the prospective nature of the relief they sought. This reversal did not reach the merits of the case, and Justice Barrett, writing for the majority, stated, "we express no view as to whether the Fifth Circuit correctly articulated the standard for when the Government transforms private conduct into state action." See *Murthy v. Missouri*, 7, n.3.

# 5

# The Dominion of God

The previous chapters have explored the relationship between political theology, political philosophy, and the sociological structure of bureaucratic systems. Here, I will address the possible elephant in the room—what does any of this have to do with Christian ethics? As the connections may not be clear to everyone, this final chapter will trace the implications of the previous chapters in light of the contours of Christian ethics.

Christian ethics (in a normative sense) is the attempt by Christians to make judgments about actions (whether mundane, extraordinary, or somewhere in between) and their ethical value in relation to theological beliefs to which they hold. Another way of asking the question posed in the previous paragraph is to replace "Christian ethics" with an area of theological thought: Incarnation, Atonement, Ecclesiology, and so on. This brings us back to Scott and Cavanaugh's possible definitions of political theology—what is theological about the political? In this context, I want to specifically focus in on Ecclesiology—as Cavanaugh has in his work on the Eucharist.

Christian ethical reflection is made up of four categories: Scripture, Tradition, Reason, and Experience.[1] I will roughly follow a similar outline for the first section of this chapter: an analysis of the Old[2] and New Testaments,[3] the development of Christian theology through important historical figures, and ending with several modern theologians and ethicists, particularly a comparison of Reinhold Niebuhr's "Christian realism" with the active pacifism of John Howard Yoder and Stanley Hauerwas. This overview may seem redundant to some readers; however, given the diversity in Christian thought, I believe it is appropriate to lay out the specific intellectual path I am tracing, rather than forcing the reader to fill in the gaps.

## OLD TESTAMENT VIEW

Before diving fully into the Old Testament, a brief discussion of higher critical development is worthy of attention. While I will not devote any space to any of the documentary source theories and variants, I do think an acknowledgment of the (apparent) tension in the concept of monotheism in the Old Testament, and its bearing on issues of sovereignty, is necessary.

The concepts of monotheism and sovereignty are similar to the paradox of the chicken and the egg—which came first? Monotheism necessitates sovereignty; if there is only one god, then that god is sovereign on the grounds of creation. However, the Old Testament narrative suggests a development of monotheism from the worship of one god (henotheism) to the understanding that there is only one god (monotheism). The conflict between divine forces mediated through human actors is indicative of this development. The gods of Egypt empowered Pharaoh's wise men to mimic certain aspects of Moses's signs—the staff turning into snakes, making water into blood. But Moses's snake-staff devours the other snakes and the entire water supply of Egypt is turned to blood. Likewise, the confrontation between Elijah and the prophets of Baal does not have Elijah deny the existence of Baal. Instead, Elijah shows Baal to be less powerful than the God of Abraham, Isaac, and Jacob through a series of rhetorical and insulting questions. At some point in the Hebrew theological development, the power of the God of Abraham, Isaac, and Jacob was understood to be so great that only one god could possess such power.[4] Hobbes's "mortal god" is similarly powerful and united. Only a singular will can form and protect the commonwealth. Other lesser powers may exist (see the development of angelology and demonology as the Old Testament progresses chronologically) but they do not have the power nor the authority to challenge God.

The Old Testament view of the State likewise develops in stages. The book of Judges describes a situation with certain parallels to what became the former thirteen colonies during the Articles of Confederation with the addition of a tribal structure. There was no centralized government to act during an invasion. The tribe whose territory was most directly threatened had to convince the other tribes that it was in their interest to intervene. Occasionally, God would raise up a "judge" (*sopet*) who would act as a military-political-religious leader for a period time.[5] The judge system "failed" when the leaders of the tribes demanded "a king for us to judge us like all the nations."[6] Samuel warns the people of the demands a king would impose upon them.[7] The books of Kings are a litany of kings who "did evil in the sight of the Lord"[8] with a few kings who "did right in the sight of the Lord"[9] sprinkled in. On the positive side, the example of King David was and remains (especially among Orthodox Jews) a messianic hope, at least when he was behaving properly.[10] For Christian theology, beginning with the writers of the Gospels, Jesus's Davidic connections were of paramount importance.

The Old Testament view of sovereignty is best expressed in the prophetic material, especially in its condemnation of idolatry. False claims of sovereignty, and the false allegiances which accompany them, are dangerous and destructive. History itself is controlled by God, even to the point of using the enemies of ancient Israel for God's own purposes. While the Israelites were God's "people," all nations are ultimately subject to God's will and purposes.[11] The particular and universal aspects of ancient Israel are a special concern of Paul in the New Testament.

## NEW TESTAMENT VIEW

God's sovereignty is assumed in the New Testament as a continuation of the Old Testament. One of the key passages (to which we will turn later, as well) is Romans 9:20-21 (a "creator as naturally sovereign over the created" argument). However, the shift in New Testament theology is the notions of power and authority in the person of Jesus. This is abundantly clear in the theological irony of the "charge" under which Jesus was put to death: "This is Jesus King of the Jews."[12] The final words of Jesus in the Gospel of Matthew (often called the Great Commission) begin with a declaration, "All authority has been given to Me in heaven and on earth."[13] Paul also connects the resurrection to Jesus's authority:

> For this reason also [Jesus's death], God highly exalted Him, and bestowed on Him the name with is above every name, so that at the name of Jesus every knee will bow, of those who are in heaven and on earth and under the earth, and that every tongue will confess that Jesus Christ is Lord, to the glory of God the Father.[14]

The image-laden Book of Revelation shows the power of Jesus over the demons and fallen angels arranged against him. Yet the problem facing Christian political thought is not the place of Jesus in political systems. The supremacy of Jesus as *the* authority is established quite early in the tradition. Instead, Christian political thought faces the problem of the application of sovereignty or authority to non-divine actors; humans. The problematic passage at the center of these interpretative disagreements is Romans 13:

> Every person is to be in subjection to the governing authorities. For there is no authority except from God, and those which exist are established by God.

Therefore whoever resists authority has opposed the ordinance of God; and they who have opposed will receive condemnation upon themselves. For rulers are not a cause of fear for good behavior, but for evil. Do you want to have no fear of authority? Do what is good and you will have praise from the same; for it is a minister of God to you for good. But if you do what is evil, be afraid; for it does not bear the sword for nothing; for it is a minister of God, an avenger who brings wrath on the one who practices evil. Therefore it is necessary to be in subjection, not only because of wrath, but also for conscience' sake. For because of this you also pay taxes, for *rulers* are servants of God, devoting themselves to this very thing. Render to all what is due them: tax to whom tax *is due;* custom to whom custom; fear to whom fear; honor to whom honor. Owe nothing to anyone except to love one another; for he who loves his neighbor has fulfilled *the* law.[15]

As Fitzmyer notes,

The passage has created a major problem in modern theological discussion because Paul's teaching has at times been invoked to justify any sort of human government. The supposition running through vv 1–7 is that the civil authorities are good and are conducting themselves rightly in seeking the interests of the political community. Paul does not envisage the possibility of either a totalitarian or a tyrannical government or one failing to cope with the just rights of individual citizens or of a minority group. He insists merely on one aspect of the question: the duty of subjects to duly constituted and legitimate authority. He does not discuss the duty or responsibility of civil authorities to the people governed, apart from one minor reference (13:4). Moreover, the concept of legitimate civil disobedience is beyond his ken.[16]

Or as Ben Witherington puts it,

Paul's advice is simple: if you do not want to live in fear, do not buck the system. When the government is functioning properly, which is what Paul seems to assume here, one who does good receives praise from the government.[17]

Paul's apparent disregard for appropriate civil disobedience has led to charges of quietism.[18] Pauline teaching seems to be of no help if the individual is good, but the government in question is evil.

The other view of the State in the New Testament comes from the Book of Revelation:

And the dragon stood on the sand of the seashore. Then I saw a beast coming up out of the sea, having ten horns and seven heads, and on his horns were ten diadems, and on his heads were blasphemous names. And the beast which I saw was like a leopard, and his feet were like those of a bear, and his mouth like the mouth of a lion. And the dragon gave him his power and his throne and great authority. I saw one of his heads as if it had been slain, and his fatal wound was healed. And the whole earth was amazed and followed after the beast; they worshiped the dragon because he gave his authority to the beast; and they worshiped the beast, saying, "Who is like the beast, and who is able to wage war with him?" There was given to him a mouth speaking arrogant words and blasphemies, and authority to act for forty-two months was given to him. And he opened his mouth in blasphemies against God, to blaspheme His name and His tabernacle, that is, those who dwell in heaven. It was also given to him to make war with the saints and to overcome them, and authority over every tribe and people and tongue and nation was given to him. All who dwell on the earth will worship him, everyone whose name has not been written from the foundation of the world in the book of life of the Lamb who has been slain. If anyone has an ear, let him hear. If anyone is destined for captivity, to captivity he goes; if anyone kills with the sword, with the sword he must be killed. Here is the perseverance and the faith of the saints. Then I saw another beast coming up out of the earth; and he had two horns like a lamb and he spoke as a dragon. He exercises all the authority of the first beast in his presence. And he makes the earth and those who dwell in it to worship the first beast, whose fatal wound was healed. He performs great signs, so that he even makes fire come down out of heaven to the earth in the presence of men. And he deceives those who dwell on the earth because of the signs which it was given him to perform in the presence of the beast, telling those who dwell on the earth to make an image to the beast who had the wound of the sword and has come to life. And it was given to him to give breath to the image of the beast, so that the image of the beast would even speak and cause as many as do not worship the image of the beast to be killed. And he causes all, the small and the great, and the rich and the poor, and the free men and the slaves, to be given a mark on their right hand or on their forehead, and he provides that no one will be able to buy or to sell, except the one who has the mark, either the name of the beast or the number of his name. Here is wisdom. Let him who has understanding calculate the number of the beast, for the number is that of a man; and his number is six hundred and sixty-six.[19]

One of the more difficult passages in Revelation, this chapter has captured the imagination of scholars and artists for millennia. Though some Christian traditions have taken this visionary experience to be literal,[20] many others understand apocalyptic literature to be purposefully subversive. The imagery is regularly connected to Rome, with the seven heads representing the seven hills of Rome. The "mark of the beast" is the gematria of Nero, who had gained a reputation as a persecutor of Christians.[21]

Paul, likely writing before the worst of Nero's reign, does not see a threat from the Roman Empire. He is able to use the mechanics of the empire to benefit his proclamation of the Gospel. John of Patmos, writing after Nero's reign, is well aware of the threat. He has seen the mechanics of the empire turned against both Christians and Jews.

God's sovereignty is also expressed through his free choice to choose Abraham, and by extension, the Jewish people.

## TRADITION

### Augustine

Nearly every topic in the Western Church begins with Augustine. From trinitarian theology, the sacraments, to ecclesiology, Augustine's writings have helped shape not only the Church but also the political concepts of Western civilization.[22] On the political side, Augustine is most known for his contributions to Just War theory, developed out of his confrontations with the Donatists. Unfortunately, purely political readings of Augustine do a great disservice to his thought by expunging the theological (and by extension, Christian ethical reasoning) in an attempt to apply Augustine to the concerns of a modern, secular world.

Augustine is not opposed to the state performing its function; however, he always mitigates such action with a purpose. Unlike the modern state, which acts for its own sake (what Foucault calls "political economy"[23]), or in democratic contexts, the presumed good of the people, Augustine is still concerned with the salvation of individual souls. On the possible execution of Donatists who murdered a Catholic priest and mutilated another, Augustine sends letters to two of the region's political leaders who were also Christians. Augustine pleads that the murderers' lives be spared. Most of the texts of the letters are concerned with retribution; Augustine does not want it to appear that the Church is taking vengeance. However, at the end of one of the letters, Augustine writes:

> They [the Donatists] did not spare the servants of God who were preaching reform to them. You should spare them when they are arrested, spare them when they are brought to you, spare them when they are convicted. They used an impious sword to shed the blood of Christians. You should prevent the sword of the law, for the sake of Christ, from shedding their blood. They killed a minister of the church and robbed him of time to live. You should allow the enemies of the church to live and have time to *repent*.[24]

In a similar letter in reference to the Donatist movement as a whole, Augustine says:

> We do not ask for vengeance on our enemies on this earth. Our sufferings ought not to constrict our spirits so narrowly that we forget the commandments given

to us, for whose truth and in whose name we suffer. We love our enemies and we pray for them. That is why we desire their reform and not their deaths, through the intervention of judges and laws that inspire fear, so that they will not meet with the punishment of everlasting judgement. We do not want you to neglect their correction; but neither do we want you to impose the punishments they deserve. Restrain their sins, therefore, in such a way that they will live to repent of having sinned.[25]

Augustine has a positive place for a theory of coercion ("judges and laws that inspire fear," "correction," "live to repent") for the State insofar as it is constructing Christian virtue. The (supposed) tension between justice and mercy is the space in which Augustine believes virtue can be cultivated. The context of Augustine's writings must be brought to the forefront. He is writing to *Christian* leaders about crimes committed against *Christians* by (in Augustine's eyes) misguided *Christians*. The State may use coercion, and perhaps even violence—note that Augustine does not deny the "sword of law" as a possible outcome for these murders; he asks that it not be applied "for the sake of Christ." The role of the Christian, according to Augustine, is to proclaim the Gospel even in the midst of that coercion and violence. This proclamation may consist of nothing more than reminding the State of its own limitations; the Church serves to remind the State that its power and apparent immortality will not last.

Most political readings of Augustine begin and end with *De civitas dei*. This is problematic given the difficulty in the metaphors Augustine uses for the relationship between the City of God and the City of Humanity.[26] Many readings suggest the two cities are in conflict and represent the redeemed and the damned, respectively. Such a reading is misguided. It is more accurate to say that the City of God and the City of Humanity are not separated by an impassable chasm. There are not two cities but only one marching through history—the City of God. The City of Humanity is, for Augustine, a mere shadow of the rebelliousness of sinful humanity against the rightful rule of God.[27] Illegitimate rebels cannot dictate to the rightful ruler, and so the City of Humanity cannot dictate to the City of God. Instead, the Church can, and at times must, speak to the State but is under no obligation to listen to the State.

## Gelasius

Based on Luke 22:38, the Two Swords Doctrine was developed in the wake of the fall of the western part of the Roman Empire, when the Church was the only institution which survived with any degree of power. The western half could have followed in the path of the Byzantines who blurred the lines between the church and the state (caesaropapism), due to the power vacuum left by the fall of Rome.[28] Instead, Pope Gelasius I "proffered a doctrine of imperial or secular rule (*regnum*) and spiritual or episcopal rule (*sacerdotium*) that laid the groundwork for subsequent thinking and controversy surrounding *ecclesia* and empires, and kingdoms and kingships."[29] By the beginning of the fourteenth century, any balance in the power of the swords was replaced by a hierarchical understanding. Pope Boniface VIII makes this explicit in his battles with the French monarchy in *Unam Sanctam*, where he "interpreted the swords as the spiritual sword wielded by the priest and the material sword wielded by kings and soldiers on behalf of and in subjection to the higher authority of the Church."[30]

The Two Swords Doctrine followed the outline of the two cities, with the *regnum* concerned with the City of Man and the *sacerdotium* concerned with the City of God. But the tension between the cities is less obvious in the Two Swords Doctrinethan in Augustine. The "two loves" which characterized each city are replaced by the change in the socio-political context. Now the Church and the State are ruled and managed by those in communion with the Catholic Church. The clear division between the cities was replaced by "Christendom" stretching from the British Isles and the Iberian Peninsula to modern Russia. The love of domination was now integrally connected with the love of God as the cities had annexed one another. While this could be interpreted as a positive, insofar as the *regnum* is now properly oriented to God as part of the *sacerdotium*, the ultimate failure of the synthesis has created difficulties in Christian political philosophy ever since.

## Aquinas

One of Aquinas's most important contributions to political theory stems from his explanation of law in the *Summa Theologica*.[31] He boils law down to "an ordinance of reason for the common good, made by him who has care of the community, and promulgated."[32] Aquinas is also aware that the law requires a coercive force for its implementation.

> [A] man is said to be subject to a law as the coerced is subject to the coercer. In this way the virtuous and righteous are not subject to the law, but only the wicked. Because coercion and violence are contrary to the will: but the will of the good is in harmony with the law, whereas the will of the wicked is discordant from it. Wherefore in this sense the good are not subject to the law, but only the wicked.[33]

This has clear connections to Paul's admonition in Romans 13. According to Aquinas, those who follow the law are not coerced, as they have assented both rationally and willfully, just as those who do good do not (or should not) need to fear the authorities.

Aquinas also seems to foreshadow Schmitt:

> The sovereign is said to be exempt from the law, as to its coercive power; since, properly speaking, no man is coerced by himself, and law has no coercive power save from the authority of the sovereign. Thus then is the sovereign said to be exempt from the law, because none is competent to pass sentence on him, if he acts against the law. Wherefore on Ps. 50:6: To Thee only have I sinned, a gloss says that there is no man who can judge the deeds of a king.—But as to the directive force of law, the sovereign is subject to the law by his own will, according to the statement . . . that whatever law a man makes for another, he should keep himself. And a wise authority says: "Obey the law that thou makest thyself." Moreover the Lord reproaches those who say and do not; and who bind heavy burdens and lay them on men's shoulders, but with a finger of their own they will not move them. Hence, in the judgment of God, the sovereign is not exempt from the law, as to its directive force; but he should fulfil it of his own free-will and not of constraint.—Again the sovereign is above the law, in so far as, when it is expedient, he can change the law, and dispense in it according to time and place.[34]

Clearly, Aquinas is not concerned with constitutional norms and states of exception in the same manner as Schmitt. The similarities in thought stem from their respective social positions. Aquinas only knows a monarchical style of government; Schmitt's fractured parliamentary system pushes him toward a strong, unitary government. And though Aquinas does have a doctrine of sin, it is isolated from other areas of the *Summa*. Each theme of the *Summa* is presented in an idealized state, freed from the corrupting effects of sin. Given the history of Israel presented in the Old Testament, Aquinas was well aware of the possibility of an evil leader.

## Luther's Two Kingdoms

Martin Luther and the Lutheran churches are often associated with the "Two Kingdoms" approach to the division between the *regnum* and *sacerdotium*. Unfortunately, Luther himself was not entirely clear on the division, and later Lutheranism compounded the lack of clarity.[35]

As shown previously, the Catholic Two Swords doctrine originally indicated that the swords work together for the common good on equal grounds, but was altered during the historical conflicts between the papacy and the French monarchs. Even under these changes, the doctrine claimed that a properly functioning secular government and a properly functioning church will both contribute to the commonwealth of the citizens. Luther is anything but that simple.

Luther's theological starting point was the received tradition of the Augustinian Order. The two kingdoms map onto the typology of *Civitas Dei*; the City of God for the "higher" things and the City of Humanity for the "lower" things. The synthesis between *sacerdotium* and *regnum* under the Two Swords doctrine was undone, leading the way for the development in Lutheran theology of a "pessimistic Augustine."[36] The Two Swords, which had been wielded in (theoretical) harmony to promote the common good, were now assigned to different spheres of life. Yet, as Augustine noted, the Christian is connected to both worlds simultaneously.[37] The Christian citizen is bound to "submit to authorities" on political issues while submitting only to Jesus in spiritual matters. Moltmann explains Luther's interpretation:

> In the realm of faith, therefore, civil pressure and political oppression must not be used. Even heretics may only be overcome by means of the Word of God and may not be politically persecuted. In the matter of faith it holds that "You must obey God more than human beings." Wherever an authority exercises religious coercion, he must be resisted. The ruler may not interfere with the kingdom of God nor with the spiritual regiment. On the other hand, the spiritual regiment may not interfere with the worldly regiment, for one cannot rule the world with the gospel. Politics is to be executed according to reason and expediency.[38]

The strict division between the secular and the spiritual has led to charges of quietism among the various forms of Protestantism which have adapted it to their own tradition. For the Lutheran tradition, this is particularly acute, given the apparent inaction in the face of the growing threat of National Socialism in Germany in the 1930s. "On the basis of the two kingdoms doctrine, the Lutheran state churches (*Landeskirchen*) maintained a 'neutral' position as documented in the Ansbach Decree of 1935."[39] But the theory (or theology) does not always enter practice in the same way:

> Whereas some Lutherans in West Germany support politically conservative powers with the help of the two kingdoms theory, Lutherans in East Germany live in and work with a state socialism by appealing to the same theory. While German Lutherans used this theory to justify favorable neutrality in the Third Reich, the Norwegian Bishop Berggrav used it to provide the rationale for his resistance against the Nazi tyranny.[40]

The difference is due to the use of what Moltmann referred to above as "reason and expediency." Reason and context must play a role in any Christian interaction with the State. Thus, the State may not encroach upon the conceptual territory of the Church, but the Church can make forays into the State through reason.[41]

## Calvin

John Calvin was a prolific writer who built upon and modified Luther's thinking. Calvin was also more consistent than Luther through his *Institutes of the Christian Religion*. Though not as long nor as theologically and philosophically rigorous as Aquinas's *Summa*, the *Institutes* represents the basic teachings of the Reformed tradition. Yet it is only in the final chapter of the final book of the *Institutes* that Calvin turns to the issue of the State.

> Having shown above that there is a twofold government in man, and having fully considered the one which, placed in the soul or inward man, relates to eternal life, we are here called to say something of the other, which pertains only to civil institutions and the external regulation of manners. For although this subject seems from its nature to be unconnected with the spiritual doctrine of faith, which I have undertaken to treat, it will appear as we proceed, that I have properly connected them, nay, that I am under the necessity of doing so, especially while, on the one hand, frantic and barbarous men are furiously endeavouring to overturn the order established by God, and, on the other, the flatterers of princes, extolling their power without measure, hesitate not to oppose it to the government of God. Unless we meet both extremes, the purity of the faith will perish.[42]

Calvin notes the two extremes that the destruction of the Two Swords doctrine freed. Both extremes elevate one of the swords while seeming to reject the other in its totality. First, the "frantic and barbarous men" are members of the Radical Reformation, or Anabaptist movement. Calvin accuses the Anabaptists of misunderstanding the "liberty" promised in the New Testament writings.

> For some, on hearing that liberty is promised in the gospel, a liberty which acknowledges no king and no magistrate among men, but looks to Christ alone, think that they can receive no benefit from their liberty so long as they see any power placed over them. Accordingly, they think that nothing will be safe until the whole world is changed into a new form, when there will be neither courts, nor laws, nor magistrates, nor anything of the kind to interfere, as they suppose, with their liberty.[43]

The *regnum* is completely undone, and only the spiritual law of Christ remains. This is a bridge too far for Calvin, who proceeds to show the necessity of the State as a check against evil (recalling Augustine's warnings on the Earthly City). On the other hand, Calvin does not wish to allow the "flatters of princes" to mislead others. Just because the prince is ordained by God (Romans 13) does not mean the prince is good. Instead, God's sovereign will is good. Calvin theologizes the problem of bad rulers with the help of the exilic stories in the Old Testament; when Israel fell away from God, a punishment was sent in the form of an oppressor.[44] The Christian is to "carry on" under such circumstances. This also seems to lead to a form of quietism, perhaps worse than that leveled at Luther. Under Luther's system, the Earthly City merely followed the rule of *libido dominandi*; humans desiring and grasping for whatever form of power was available. Calvin's system does not change this desiring and grasping but seems to give it divine permission. Evil rulers grasp for power, but God has sent them to punish the wicked through such desire for power. The theo-ethical dilemma is one of first causes. Calvin sees the difficulty in this position but is once again able to turn to the Old Testament to create a space for resistance. Oppressive rulers are overthrown often: Pharaoh by Moses is the clearest example, though the entire book of Judges serves as a collection of mini-examples. For Calvin, God acts to overthrow evil rulers once they have fulfilled their purpose as a punishment from God. But how does God act?

> Although the Lord takes vengeance on unbridled domination, let us not therefore suppose that that vengeance is committed to us, to whom no command has been given but to obey and suffer. I speak only of private men. For when popular magistrates have been appointed to curb the tyranny of kings (as the Ephori, who were opposed to kings among the Spartans, or Tribunes of the people to consuls among the Romans, or Demarchs to the senate among the Athenians; and perhaps there is something similar to this in the power exercised in each kingdom by the three orders, when they hold their primary diets).[45]

One of Calvin's most interesting comments comes not from the *Institutes* but from his commentary on Numbers. There, the priest Phinehas kills an Israelite man and his Midianite female companion for violating God's command to not consort with the Midianites.[46] After explaining why Phinehas is praised by God, Calvin notes,

> Now, if any private person should in his preposterous zeal take upon himself to punish a similar crime, in vain will he boast that he is an imitator of Phinehas, unless he shall be thoroughly assured of the command of God.[47]

A private citizen, that is, anyone who is not a magistrate, may not take matters into their own hands, whether the crime is adultery or tyranny. Calvin does not seem to believe that anyone would be arrogant enough to claim such assurance unless God would, somehow, praise them *post facto*.

Calvin's high view of God's sovereignty and power forces him to argue that rulers, whom God has appointed, must be obeyed, insofar as they do not force the citizen to sin. Yet at no point is a private citizen allowed to take up arms against an unrighteous ruler unless God has clearly commanded it. Other public citizens, however, likely in the form of lesser magistrates or other titles which had some degree of authority over aspects of the State, could act as it was their duty to protect the commonwealth just as much as it had been the now-wicked king's duty. This suggests that some authority is proper further down the chain of power. Yet Calvin's entire structure indicates that the State may use coercion and violence because God has appointed the State as part of the divine plan.

## Wesley

John Wesley was the last of the great Protestant Reformers, though several centuries removed. Wesley's Church of England had broken from the Roman Catholic Church two centuries previously. The break was less about theology per se and dealt more with long-standing tension between Pope and Monarch in the late Medieval period. As Wesley was not attempting to convince German princes of their role in the "Two Kingdoms" nor attempting to create a new commonwealth based on Reformed principles, his political writings appeared as tracts devoted to a particular issue at a particular time. The most famous is his condemnation of the American War for Independence, *A Calm Address to Our American Colonies*.[48] This tract was an abridgment and rewriting of Samuel Johnson's *Taxation No Tyranny*.[49] It is difficult to say how much of Wesley's original thought is in *Calm Address*, but his decision to print it under his name suggests his agreement with Johnson's main points.[50]

The concern of Wesley (and Johnson) was the colonists' cry of "no taxation without representation." The colonial charters had not given the colonists the right to parliamentary representatives, so they were in fact members of a corporation subject to the King. Wesley states, "Considering this, nothing can be more plain, than that the supreme power in England has a legal right of laying any tax upon them for any end beneficial to the whole empire."[51] This transitions into a discussion of political theory. Wesley turns against the Lockean concept of consent, a fundamental aspect of the Lockean social contract theory. Representation undoes most theories of consent, in that I do not directly consent to the laws passed, perhaps especially if I voted for the opposition party. But more so, "how has any man consented to those laws, which were made before he was born? Our consent to these, nay and to the laws now made even in England, is purely passive."[52]

The broadside against Lockean principles continues in an argument-counterargument progression:

> But you say, You *are intitled to life, liberty and property by nature: and that you have never ceded to any sovereign power, the right to dispose of these without your consent.*
> While you speak as the naked sons of nature, this is certain true. . . . You are no longer in a state of nature, but sink down to Colonists, governed by a charter. If your ancestors were subjects, the acknowledged a Sovereign: if they had a right to English privileges, they were accountable to English laws, and had *ceded* to the King and Parliament, *the power of disposing without their consent*, of both *their lives, liberties and properties.*[53]

The language of ceding rights, along with the anti-Lockean sentiments, suggests (at the least) a quasi-Hobbesian political theory (which further implies a Schmittian understanding of sovereignty, as I have suggested previously). Citizens do not actively consent to a social contract but are born into a system in which political authority has already been established. Citizens are not asked at the age of majority whether they "consent" to each and every law. Instead, new citizens are absorbed into the realm of the Leviathan.

## The Modern Problem

Unfortunately, the previous discussions of important Christian thinkers are complicated by their relationship to pre-bureaucratic thinking. The difficulty in Christian political theory is the intellectual leap from an ancient Roman province or an early modern German fiefdom to contemporary Washington, Paris, or London. The Enlightenment highlights parts of this difficulty. The rediscovery of Plato, Aristotle, and other classical sources in the lead-up to the European Renaissance was not a simple transition. The "democracy" of the Greek city-states could only be replicated at the level of the free cities interspersed within the Holy Roman Empire. The attempts of thinkers we covered in chapter 1 to widen such democratic systems to countries of the size and cultural/ethnic differences such as absolutist France were doomed to fail. The conflicts of the Glorious Revolution and the French Revolution were the necessary outcomes of the power struggles between the monarchy and the representatives of the People.

Given the this-worldliness of politics and the "violence inherent in the system"[54] it is not surprising that a wing of the Church would develop a theopolitics rejecting such aspects. The destruction of the radical Anabaptists led to the development of the Mennonite movement. Of this intellectual history, the contributions of John Howard Yoder[55] and Stanley Hauerwas stand as a challenge to the "Constantinian" model which allows for various formulations of Church/State interaction.

As with other topics in this study, a review of definitions is important. Theodore J. Koontz lays out a helpful conceptual differentiation between "pacifism," "abolitionism," and "nonviolent resistance." Pacifism relies on the sharp dichotomy between the Church and State; pacifism "is—minimally—the view that it is *morally* wrong for *me* to participate *directly* in *killing* in *all war*" while the correlative maximal view is that "it is morally wrong for *everyone, all* killing is wrong, etc."[56] In such a model, the two swords or two kingdoms are irrevocably separated (minimal) or the *sacerdotium* rules fully over the *regnum* (maximal). The minimal position was the historic position of the Anabaptists as laid out in the Schleitheim Confession:

> *Sixth, concerning the sword:* The sword is ordained of God outside the perfection of Christ. It punishes and puts to death the wicked, and guards and protects the good. In the Law the sword was ordained for the punishment of the wicked and for their death, and the same [sword] is [now] ordained to be used by the worldly magistrates. In the perfection of Christ, however, only the ban is used for a warning and for the excommunication of the one who has sinned, without putting the flesh to death,—simply the warning and the command to sin no more. Now it will be asked by many who do not recognize [this as] the will of Christ for us, whether a Christian may or should employ the sword against the wicked for the defence and protection of the good, or for the sake of love.[57]

Magistrates do have God-given authority to wield the sword, but Christians may not wield the sword; thus, Christians may not be magistrates.[58] However, in a democratic society in which individuals can attempt to influence governmental positions, and the possibility of nuclear war, the maximal view has gradually become the standard from which Anabaptists operate. The crucial point is that minimal pacifism accepts the coercive nature of the State and declines to participate in it. Abolitionism borders on utopianism in the belief that war can be abolished through "a confidence in human nature (apart from conversion) and in education—helping people see the evident follies and costs of war as a means of settling conflicts," which does not require a Christian community, merely an enlightened human community.[59] Nonviolent resistance is best illustrated by Gandhi in the Indian-British colonial situation and his influence on King in the American Civil Rights Movement. These were the only modern "wins" for nonviolent resistance at the time of Yoder's writing. Minimal pacifism worked for those communities that followed it, given that they were "protected" by non-pacifistic "magistrates."

Abolitionism, in its form as the League of Nations, had failed spectacularly, and the United Nations was ineffective in halting the Cold War. No independent society has yet achieved maximal pacifism.[60]

This reality makes the intellectual explorations of Yoder and Hauerwas all the more important, as we have no historical model on which to debate the merits. Yoder's *Politics of Jesus* is as foundational to the Christian pacifist movement as Gutiérrez's *A Theology of Liberation* is to liberation theologies. Yoder's project is complicated, however, by his focus on the person of Jesus.[61] That is, Yoder takes the first of Ramsey's sources of authority, Scripture, and elevates a part of that, the Gospels, above the rest. Tradition, Reason, and Experience are not completely forgotten, but each is drastically reduced in importance.

Stanley Hauerwas took Yoder's focus on Christian discipleship and applied it to the community of the Church. Hauerwas's body of work follows a narrative of rise-decline-hope. The early Church rejected the Empire and reoriented toward the risen Christ. Unfortunately, so the narrative goes, the Church and Empire were merged under Constantine in a process by which the Church gives legitimacy to the "secular" governing structures in exchange for participation in the power of those structures.[62] This arrangement led to "Christendom" in Europe and is often pejoratively called "Constantinianism." But hope remains in the fact that American Christianity has lost its place of cultural prestige. Now the Church can be true to its calling: "The decline of the old, Constantinian synthesis between the church and the world means that we American Christians are at last free to be faithful in a way that makes being a Christian today an exciting adventure."[63] Yet Hauerwas is not calling for the withdrawal from society and culture, a return to anchoritic desert living or the quasi-monastic "Benedict Option" proposed by Rod Dreher.[64] He is instead calling for the creation of a new society and culture through a return to the political claim of the first Christians, "Christ is Lord."

In fact, Hauerwas is one of the few Christian thinkers to note a problem between the State and bureaucracy. While I am in agreement with Hauerwas and the sources he uses, I want to draw special attention to the ways in which we are highlighting different aspects of the problem; I will break up his long discussion surrounding bureaucracy with my own comments to do so.

> As Lesslie Newbigin has pointed out, at the core of our culture is an ideal of knowledge of what are called "the facts." These wonderful entities can become even more impressive as "data" when given particular authority through the pseudo-methodologies of the social sciences. They are allegedly quite independent of the "subjective biases" of the knower. They are therefore "value-free."[65]

Hauerwas focuses on the use of "data" (see chapter 2 for my discussion) in the social sciences. His distaste for the "soft sciences" is quite clear. Yet he goes on to say:

> But it is a mistake to think that scientific methodologies gave birth to the expert. Rather it was the necessity of liberal societies to find social mechanisms to provide for social control—bureaucracy being the seminal cause for this—that creates the necessity of facts over which experts can be authorities. For bureaucracies are built as mechanical models where a high degree of division of labor, specialization, predictability, and anonymity are meant to ensure the criterion of efficiency.[66]

Hauerwas is an ethicist and theologian, not a sociological historian like Weber. Thus, his historical account is questionable. Bureaucratic thinking appeared apart from the needs of liberal society (one of Hauerwas's regular objects of scorn). The move toward the rationalization of thought influenced both the development of bureaucratic systems and the structure of liberal (in a Rawlsian sense) norms. However, it is not readily apparent that this historical error renders his larger argument void.

> Bureaucracy is legitimated by its promise to be efficient and effective. The figure who reigns supreme in this world is, of course, the manager who is supported by social scientists. Just as theologians once were in the service of bishops, popes, and kings, now social scientists are used to legitimate our leaders who promise to be the best managers of crisis.[67]

Here we see Hauerwas's affinity for MacIntyre quite clearly through his introduction of the figure of the manager into a context in which it had not appeared. It also creates some confusion—are the "leaders" politicians who rely on managers, or are the "leaders" managers who rely on social scientists? The former seems the more likely of the two, but the move from bureaucracy to its personalized form in the shape of the manager complicates the picture. Still, this gives us another look at the secularization process; even advice has been desacralized by the move toward rationalization.

> To underwrite the authority of such experts, to ensure their predictive power, it is necessary to create the fact-value distinction. In fact we increasingly become self-interested individuals to ensure our new master's authorities for otherwise we fear anarchy. In short, it becomes a moral necessity to be greedy as otherwise we would throw people out of work, and the predictive power of economics would be even more doubtful than it already is.[68]

The leap from "fact-value" to "greed" as a shorthand for capitalism and thus the American economy is a wide one, assuming that the "we" in this section are Americans (or members of a liberal society) and not Christians.

> It has become a commonplace that one of the oddities of modernity has been how societies built on claims of the freedom of the individual, with the attending distinction between the public and private, have led to the growth of the bureaucratic state. Of course such a state appears noncoercive, since its task is not to compel obedience, but rather to achieve administrative ends. The state is putatively in existence to protect individual rights, but to accomplish that end it is necessary to create a bureaucracy that is more intrusive than the most absolute monarch.[69]

This is the point at which my inquiry and Hauerwas's concerns are most in sync. Liberalism as a political-philosophical system in which individual rights are protected from others and the State (Locke) contains an inner contradiction of violence, power, and value-neutral rhetorics in the name of justice. State-centered bureaucracies exist to facilitate the power of the State in the defense of rights and furthering the "pursuit of happiness" in both domestic and foreign contexts. Thus, the Department of Defense and other aspects of the national security umbrella (generally) attempt to protect the "rights" of American citizens against foreign violence. Likewise, the Department of Treasury (generally) attempts to build up the US economy for the good of all citizens. Unfortunately, one of the most efficient ways to protect Americans is through mass surveillance, to say nothing of the morally questionable activities which happen abroad. And the most efficient way to help the economy is to target its greatest gains at the upper-middle and upper classes, where a percentage rate in tax reductions has a noticeable change. Both of these positions are associated with the conservative side of politics, but examples could be given from the progressive side as well. Efficiency in K-12 education requires the ending of private and homeschool options in that all students are educated under the same standards, with teachers trained to the same standards, with no outliers who may be unfit (or overly competent). Liberal governments must use some form of power, coercion, or violence to achieve these standards of "rights" and "justice." Incentivization understood as the carrot aspect of the stick-and-carrot metaphor, cannot keep a country permanently safe. Social engineering through tax breaks and other bonuses is generally arbitrary and actually go against the value-neutral perspective which liberal systems are to operate from. The option to file separately or jointly for married couples in the United States falls into this category. The Tax Policy Center, a collaboration between the Urban Institute and the Brookings Institute, highlights two aspects of this phenomenon:

Couples in which spouses have similar incomes are more likely to incur marriage penalties than couples in which one spouse earns most of the income, because combining incomes in joint filing can push both spouses into higher tax brackets.

Couples in which one spouse earns all or most of a couple's income rarely incur a marriage penalty and almost always receive a marriage bonus because joint filing shifts the higher earner's income into a lower tax bracket.[70]

Though unstated, such a policy favors families in which one spouse works part-time and cares for the children while the other works full-time. This tracks with classic conceptions of the nuclear family in the (white) American psyche, with the addition of taking the reality of two-income families as a necessity in the neoliberal context (see chapter 5 on neoliberalism). Both the stick (coercion) and the carrot (value-biased social engineering) are problematic to liberal societies as each violates a core aspect of the liberal understanding of individual rights and a rejection of a "common good" beyond allowing everyone individually to seek their own conception of the "good." The carrot approach is more suitable to Christian conceptions through the rejection of value-neutral standards but still does not get us to the point of a "Christian" State.

On the possibility of a Christian state, it seems that Yoder and Hauerwas may have more in common with Augustine than we would expect at first glance. We do not know Augustine's views on whether Christians *should* be in service of the State; the conversion of Constantine and the subsequent acceptance of Christianity as the religion of the Empire had occurred long before Augustine's birth. However, it is likely that Augustine would agree with Yoder and Hauerwas that there could not be a "Christian" state; the State's requirement to "wield the sword" makes a thoroughly Christian commonwealth an impossibility. However, it is undeniable that Augustine was thoroughly Constantinian. The difference between the systems of thought is one of purity. Yoder and Hauerwas claim that the State is so corrupted by sin, taking the form of hubris and violence, that nothing good can come from it. This position is akin to the Donatists of Augustine's day in that otherwise well-meaning Christians (priests who had not been *traditors* but were ordained by bishops who had been *traditors*) are impure because of their connection to the others (the *traditors*). According to the Donatists, the sacraments performed by such ordained priests were ineffective and invalid. Arguments over purity are common in the history of Christianity, and in religion more generally.[71] Augustine would certainly accept the validity of sacraments carried out by military chaplains. I am unaware of any statements by Hauerwas on this topic.[72]

In this discussion of purity, it only seems right to move to a Christian thinker who outright rejected purity claims, Reinhold Niebuhr. In an interview with David Brooks, an op-ed columnist for the *New York Times*, then-Senator and Democratic presidential primary candidate Barack Obama expressed his admiration for Reinhold Niebuhr. In response to Brooks's question on Niebuhr:

> "I take away," Obama answered in a rush of words, "the compelling idea that there's serious evil in the world, and hardship and pain. And we should be humble and modest in our belief we can eliminate those things. But we shouldn't use that as an excuse for cynicism and inaction. I take away . . . the sense we have to make these efforts knowing they are hard, and not swinging from naïve idealism to bitter realism."[73]

We will leave aside for a moment the question of whether Yoder and Hauerwas fit the "naïve idealism" side. Niebuhr avoids the "bitter realism" by formulating "Christian realism"—a realism grounded in Christian theology.

Niebuhr, like his Swiss counterpart Karl Barth, was troubled by the direction of early twentieth-century Liberal Protestantism. Liberal Protestantism had merged Jesus the Teacher with the concept of the evolutionary progression of society. The kingdom of God was possible on Earth and would come about as humanity progressed into more moral beings. Niebuhr rejected such conclusions:

> The man on the cross turned defeat into victory and prophesied the day when love would be triumphant in the world. But the triumph would have to come through the intervention of God. The moral resources of men would not be sufficient to guarantee it. A sentimental generation has destroyed this apocalyptic note in the vision of the Christ. It thinks the kingdom of God is around the corner, while he regarded it as impossible of realisation, except by God's grace.[74]

Niebuhr is expressing the "already/not-yet" tension in the New Testament. Christ has *already* brought the kingdom of God to Earth, but it is *not yet* fulfilled or consummated. Such fulfillment requires the apocalyptic, that is, the "revealing" as the word originally meant, act of God. Humanity cannot build the kingdom of God on Earth any more than they succeeded in building the Tower of Babel. The "War to End All Wars" (a human inversion of the apocalyptic Battle of Armageddon) had shown that humanity was not progressing. In fact, humanity may have slipped a few rungs on the ladder of progress in the no man's land between the trenches in the French countryside. The Liberal idealism which had become part and parcel of the mainline Christianity of America was severely damaged by the war. Whatever was left of it was utterly destroyed, along with the ladder of human progression, at Auschwitz and Dachau, Hiroshima and Nagasaki. Technological progress was not a salvific route when humanity was still flawed—it merely resulted in more death and destruction.

This leads to Niebuhr's other line of attack on Liberal Protestantism, the doctrine of original sin. Part of Niebuhr's connection to the doctrine of original sin comes from the misattribution of the quote "The doctrine of original sin is the only empirically verifiable doctrine in the Christian faith" to Niebuhr when he had simply "approvingly quoted . . . from the London *Times Literary Supplement*."[75] Niebuhr's brief contemporary G. K. Chesterton, a devout Catholic, similarly quipped, "Certain new theologians dispute original sin, which is the only part of Christian theology which can really be proved."[76] Though Niebuhr "interpreted Genesis allegorically,"[77] thus rejecting a literal Adam, Eve, and snake, he still accepted the reality of sin as a pervasive and inescapable power in both individual lives and societies. Individuals could be saved from sin through the grace of God, but societies were unable to be free of the effects of sin, hence the title of one of Niebuhr's more popular works: *Moral Man and Immoral Society*. Societies are political things, and as politics is concerned with power, no society could truly escape the clutches of self-interest the same way Christians are commanded to take up a life of *agape* love.[78] It is, in fact, an impossibility for States to have any ethical stances as States under Niebuhr's thinking since

> the nation is a corporate unity, held together much more by force and emotion, than by mind. Since there can be no ethical action without self-criticism, and no self-criticism without the rational capacity of self-transcendence, it is natural that national attitudes can hardly approximate the ethical.[79]

Because States are collections of individuals who may have nothing more in common than their shared citizenship, and that democracies have the added complication of the fiction of popular sovereignty, self-criticism is nonsensical. It may be that certain aspects of the State are capable of State-focused self-criticism, but these are rarely the parts of the State that are in power. It is much easier for opposition parties or media commentators to engage in self-criticism because it is not really *self*-criticism because there is no ownership of the actions being critiqued. There is a disconnected space between the individual and the actions of the State in which the necessary fictions of sovereignty begin to crack.

We now have the poles of the debate in Christian political thought sketched out.[80] On one side we have the Augustinian division of the Cities, with the Two Swords (and later systems based on the *sacerdotium/regnum* division) providing an apparent synthesis of the City of God and the City of Humanity.

On the other, we see the Yoder/Hauerwas claim of an alternative political system that exists as a condemnation of State power and a way of escaping complicity with that system. The foundational assumptions of each side on the nature of the State prevent a reconciliation between the poles. Both systems seem to be internally consistent from both a theological and philosophical standpoint.

## NOTES

1. This four-part structure was popularized in modern ethics by Paul Ramsey.
2. As this study works within the Christian tradition, I will retain the Christianized title.
3. As a matter of biblical interpretation, I will use a "face value" approach; neither always "literal" nor always "metaphorical" but an attempt to let the authors' voices come through as much as possible before turning to interpretative methods and theories. Though other forms of interpretation are possible, I believe part of the disconnect between academic Christian ethics and practitioners (many of whom have never heard the name Wellhausen or the nuances of Markan priority) is our (that is, academics) inability to return to the text as read by the average church-goer. The tension between the Academy and Church begins with method and theory, and attempts to lessen that tension must start here.
4. Walter Brueggemann, *Old Testament Theology: An Introduction* (Nashville, TN: Abingdon Press, 2008), 121–156.
5. Consider the parallel with Roman history in the person of Cincinnatus, who relinquished power after the resolution of the conflict, and the antitype of Julius Caesar.
6. I Samuel 8:5. All biblical citations are from the New American Standard Bible.
7. I Samuel 8:10-22. For an overview of Samuel's discussions on the future monarchy, see David Toshio Tsumura, *The First Book of Samuel*, New International Commentary on the Old Testament (Grand Rapids, MI: William B. Eerdmans Pub. Co., 2007), 247–261.
8. For example, I Kings 14:22
9. For example, I Kings 15:10
10. For example, Psalm 122:5 and Isaiah 9:7. David's two problematic points were the incident with Bathsheba and the census of the people in 2 Samuel 24:1-25 and I Chronicles 21. On Bathsheba, see April D. Westbrook, *'And He Will Take Your Daughters . . .': Woman Story and the Ethical Evaluation of Monarchy in the David Narrative* (New York: Bloomsbury T&T Clark, 2015), 113–141; and on the census, see Ralph W. Klein, *1 Chronicles*, Hermeneia (Minneapolis, MN: Fortress Press, 2006), 414–427.
11. See Jon N. Oswalt, *The Book of Isaiah: Chapters 1-39*, New International Commentary on the Old Testament (Grand Rapids, MI: William B. Eerdmans Pub. Co., 1998), 34–36.

12. Matthew 27:37. The entire trial and crucifixion are presented (in Matthew) in ironic terms in that the Jewish leadership was unable to recognize Jesus as King but the Romans are closer to the truth through their mocking.

13. Matthew 28:18b.

14. Philippians 2:9-11. See also Oscar Cullmann, *The Christology of the New Testament*, trans. Shirley C. Guthrie and Charles A. M. Hall, Revised (Philadelphia, PA: The Westminster Press, 1963), 195–237, esp. 200; and Nijay K. Gupta and Fredrick J. Long, "The Politics of Ephesians and the Empire: Accommodation or Resistance?" *Journal of Greco-Roman Christianity & Judaism* 7 (January 2010): 112–136. Other early Christian titles for Jesus (e.g., savior) may also have a political dimension as anti-emperor appellations.

15. Romans 13:1-9 (The NASB uses italics for words which are implied by the context but do not appear explicitly in the original language); see James D. G. Dunn, "Romans 13:1-7: A Charter for Political Quietism?," *Ex Auditu* 2 (1986): 55–68 for a contextualization in historical and literary themes of Romans 13 with the rest of the epistle.

16. Joseph A. Fitzmyer, *Romans: A New Translation with Introduction and Commentary* (New Haven, CT: Yale University Press, 1993), 665. Problematically, Fitzmyer is reading "just rights" and "minority group" back into the first century.

17. Ben Witherington III and Darlene Hyatt, *Paul's Letter to the Romans: A Socio-Rhetorical Commentary* (Grand Rapids, MI: Eerdmans Publishing, 2004), 313.

18. See Dunn.

19. Revelation 13:1-18.

20. Revelation 1:10, "I was in the Spirit" likely means a vision from the Holy Spirit.

21. Craig R. Koester argues persuasively for such an interpretation in his "The Number of the Beast in Revelation 13 in Light of Papyri, Graffiti, and Inscriptions," *Journal of Early Christian History* 6, no. 3 (2016), esp. 9–13.

22. Peter Brown's *Augustine of Hippo: A Biography*, New (Oakland, CA: University of California Press, 2000) is still recognized as the standard account of Augustine's life.

23. Michel Foucault, *The Birth of Biopolitics: Lectures at the* College de France, *1978-79*, ed. Michel Senellart, trans. Graham Burchell (New York: Palgrave MacMillian, 2008), 13–19.

24. Augustine, Letter 134 in *Augustine: Political Writings*, ed. E. M. Atkins and R. J. Dodaro (Cambridge, MA: Cambridge University Press, 2004).

25. Ibid., Letter 100.

26. Augustine uses variations on *terrenae ciuitatis* ("earthly city") more than *hominum ciuitatis* (the older "city of man" or "city of humanity"). Thematically, however, it would be more accurate to call the cities by their loves: The City of the Love of God and the City of the Love of Domination (*dominandi libido*), where domination means the attempt to bend others to one's own will and desires.

27. Augustine's Neoplatonism shows through in these types of contexts as "the Real" is distorted into shadows on the wall of a cave.

28. This blurring continued in Eastern Orthodox countries, even through the twentieth century in the form of national churches becoming a wing of the state (Greece, Russia in both its pre- and post-Soviet versions, and to a degree, even during the Soviet era). The fascinating aspect of this tendency is that it pre-dates the Christian era. Alexander the Great is recognized as a god as he moves further east into Asia Minor, a development which would have lasting impacts on the Greco-Roman world (e.g., Antiochus Epiphanes in Judea and the deification of Julius Caesar after his assassination). There are indications that the cult of the Roman emperor was stronger in the east than it was in Rome itself. The degree to which this tendency can be tracked to a deeper cause is, however, unclear. On these issues see Ittai Gradel, *Emperor Worship and Roman Religion* (New York: Oxford University Press, 2002), Hans-Josef Klauck, *The Religious Context of Early Christianity: A Guide to Graeco-Roman Religions* (Minneapolis, MN: Fortress Press, 2003) and Cullmann, 195–199.

29. Jean Bethke Elshtain, *Sovereignty: God, State, and Self* (New York: Basic Books, 2008), 11.

30. Christopher Roy Hutson, "Enough for What?: Playacting Isaiah 53 in Luke 22:35-38," *Restoration Quarterly* 55, no. 1 (2013): 39; see 36–43 for an overview of the abundance of possible interpretations.

31. Thomas Aquinas, *Summa Theologica* (London: Burns Oates & Washbourne Fathers of the English Dominican Province, 1912). Sometimes referred to as the "Treatise on Law" this topic runs from II.i., q. 90–q. 108.

32. Ibid., II.i., q. 90, resp.

33. Ibid., II.i., q. 96, resp.

34. Ibid., II.i., q. 96, ad. 3.

35. Jürgen Moltmann, *On Human Dignity: Political Theology and Human Rights* (Minneapolis, MN: Fortress Press, 1987), 63.

36. The phrase comes from Lisa Sowle Cahill, "Sovereign No More? Selves, States, and God in Our Bewildering Global Environment," in *Jean Bethke Elshtain: Politics, Ethics, and Society*, ed. Debra Erickson and Michael Le Chevallier (Notre Dame, IN: Notre Dame University Press, 2018). 139. Bethke was Lutheran until her late-in-life conversion to Catholicism.

37. The traditional Johannine corpus of the New Testament is the grounding of this notion.

38. Moltmann, 70. Inner quotations are from Luther.

39. Moltmann, 61.

40. Ibid., 63.

41. Though both Luther and Calvin are more pessimistic about the functioning of human reason, both give some space to forms of natural law argumentation, which allows for a degree of correspondence between human reason and divine reason.

42. John Calvin, *Institutes of the Christian Religion*, trans. Henry Beveridge (Bellingham, WA: Logos Bible Software, 1997), IV, xx, i.

43. Ibid.

44. Ibid., IV, xx, xxv–xxxii.

45. Ibid., IV, xx, xxxi.

46. Numbers 25:1-18. It is possible that there is a sexual pun taking place at the moment of the killings. Phinehas drives a spear through the man and the woman simultaneously, with particular emphasis that it pierced her "belly." Given the necessary proximity and angles, it is likely that Phinehas killed them during *coitus*, possibly going through the man's back and out his genital region to penetrate the woman's stomach. This passage and interpretation were pointed out to me by both John Kelsay and Martin Kavka on separate occasions.

47. John Calvin, *Commentaries on the Four Last Books of Moses Arranged in the Form of a Harmony*, trans. Charles William Bingham, 4 vols. (Edinburgh: Calvin Translation Society, 1852).

48. John Wesley, *A Calm Address to Our American Colonies* (London: R. Hawes, 1775), https://archive.org/details/calmaddresstoour00wesl.

49. Glen O'Brien, "John Wesley's Rebuke to the Rebels of British America: Revisiting the *Calm Address*," *Methodist Review* 4 (2012): 35.

50. Ibid. See also Thomas W. Smith, "Authority and Liberty: John Wesley's View of Medieval England," *Wesley and Methodist Studies* 7, no. 1 (2015): 5, on Wesley's reprinting of other works.

51. Wesley, 4.

52. Ibid., 6.

53. Ibid., 3–4. Emphasis original.

54. Terry Gillam and Terry Jones, *Monty Python and the Holy Grail* (EMI Films, 1975).

55. On Yoder: Just as any work dealing with Carl Schmitt must address his affiliation with the Nazis, so any work dealing with John Howard Yoder must address his sexual harassment of women under the guise of "theological experimentation." The definitive record is Rachel Waltner Goosen, "'Defanging the Beast': Mennonite Responses to John Howard Yoder's Sexual Abuse," *Mennonite Quarterly Review* 89 (January 2015): 7–80. There, she quotes from a piece by Brian Hamilton and Kyle Lambelet, who "argue that scholars have a continuing responsibility to interrogate Yoder's theological work with his history of sexual violence in mind. This includes not only his writings on human sexuality, but more importantly, his writings on peace and nonviolence." I bring this to the forefront to acknowledge that I am deficient in this area and must apologize in advance for any aspects of Yoder's thought which connect to his grotesque behavior that I do not point out. Just as with Schmitt, I do not seek to rehabilitate Yoder the man; I merely seek to investigate his political thought insofar as it bears on this study.

56. Theodore J. Koontz, "Christian Nonviolence: An Interpretation," in *Christian Political Ethics*, ed. John A. Coleman (Princeton, NJ: Princeton University Press, 2008), 233. Emphasis original.

57. The article continues: "Our reply is unanimously as follows: Christ teaches and commands us to learn of Him, for He is meek and lowly in heart and so shall we find rest to our souls. Also Christ says to the heathenish woman who was taken in adultery, not that one should stone her according to the law of His Father (and yet He says, As the Father has commanded me, thus I do), hut *[sic]* in mercy and forgiveness and

warning, to sin no more. Such [an attitude] we also ought to take completely according to the rule of the ban.

Secondly, it will be asked, whether a Christian shall pass sentence in worldly disputes and strife such as unbelievers have with one another. This is our united answer: Christ did not wish to decide or pass judgment between brother and brother in the case of the inheritance, but refused to do so. Therefore we should do likewise.

Thirdly, it will be asked concerning the sword, Shall one be a magistrate if one should be chosen as such? The answer is as follows: They wished to make Christ king, but He fled and did not view it as the arrangement of His Father. Thus shall we do as He did, and follow Him, and so shall we not walk in darkness. For He Himself says, He who wishes to come after me, let him deny himself and take up his cross and follow me. Also, He Himself forbids the [employment of] the force of the sword saying, The worldly princes lord it over them, etc., but not so shall it be with you. Further, Paul says, Whom God did foreknow He also did predestinate to be conformed to the image of His Son, etc. Also Peter says, Christ has suffered (not ruled) and left us an example, that ye should follow His steps.

Finally it will be observed that it is not appropriate for a Christian to serve as a magistrate because of these points: The government magistracy is according to the flesh, but the Christians' is according to the Spirit; their houses and dwelling remain in this world, but the Christians' are in heaven; their citizenship is in this world, but the Christians' citizenship is in heaven; the weapons of their conflict and war are carnal and against the flesh only, but the Christians' weapons are spiritual, against the fortification of the devil. The worldlings are armed with steel and iron, but the Christians are armed with the armor of God, with truth, righteousness, peace, faith, salvation and the Word of God." J. C. Wenger, trans., "Schleitheim Confession of the Swiss Brethren," *The Mennonite Quarterly Review* XIX, no. 4 (October 1945): 247–253.

58. See John Howard Yoder, *The Politics of Jesus: Vicit Agnus Noster*, 2nd ed. (Grand Rapids, MI: William B. Eerdmans, 1994), 198.

59. Koontz, 234.

60. The few countries with no standing militaries are protected through a series of formal and informal agreements. All have some form of domestic police force. See Amanda Macias, "From Aruba to Iceland, These 36 Nations Have No Standing Military," *CNBC*, April 3, 2018, https://www.cnbc.com/2018/04/03/countries-that-do-not-have-a-standing-army-according-to-cia-world-factbook.html.

61. Gutiérrez is undertaking a constructive theology, Yoder is trying to make sense of biblical, historical, and constructive theologies.

62. Stanley Hauerwas and William H. Willimon, *Resident Aliens* (Nashville, TN: Abingdon Press, 1989), 27.

63. Ibid., 18.

64. Rod Dreher, *The Benedict Option: A Strategy for Christians in a Post-Christian Nation* (New York: Sentinel, 2018).

65. Stanley Hauerwas, *After Christendom?: How the Church Is to Behave If Freedom, Justice, and a Christian Nation Are Bad Ideas* (Nashville, TN: Abingdon Press, 1999), 63.

66. Ibid., 64.
67. Ibid.
68. Ibid., 64–65.
69. Ibid., 65–66.
70. "What Are Marriage Penalties and Bonuses?," *Tax Policy Center*, https://www.taxpolicycenter.org/briefing-book/what-are-marriage-penalties-and-bonuses (Accessed February 10, 2020).
71. The legal codes in the Pentateuch, the prophetic denunciation of idol worship as adultery, Jesus's interactions with sinners, and the circumcision debate in Acts 15 are a few examples merely from the biblical account. The prime examples from church history are the Reformers, especially those in the decades before Luther, such as Jan Hus. The standard text on "purity" in religious studies is Mary Douglas, *Purity and Danger: An Analysis of Concept of Pollution and Taboo* (London: Routledge, 2002).
72. The best reference I can find to military chaplains comes from an anecdote Hauerwas gave as a part of a commencement speech to Eastern Mennonite Seminary, see Stanley Hauerwas, "Speaking Christian: A Commencement Address for Eastern Mennonite Seminary," *Mennonite Quarterly Review* 84, no. 3 (July 2010): 41–49.
73. David Brooks, "Obama, Gospel and Verse," *The New York Times*, April 26, 2007, http://www.nytimes.com/2007/04/26/opinion/26brooks.html.
74. Reinhold Niebuhr, *Moral Man and Immoral Society: A Study in Ethics and Politics*, 2nd ed. (Louisville, KY: John Knox Press, 2013), 82.
75. Andrew S. Finstuen, *Original Sin and Everyday Protestants: The Theology of Reinhold Niebuhr, Billy Graham, and Paul Tillich in an Age of Anxiety* (Chapel Hill, NC: The University of North Carolina Press, 2009), 69.
76. Gilbert K. Chesterton, *Orthodoxy* (New York: John Lane Company, 1908), 24.
77. Finstuen, 70.
78. Ibid., 83–112. It is due to this understanding that Niebuhr adopted "Christian Realism" as his view on international affairs during the Cold War, where "realism" is the school of thought that claims nations will act in their own self-interests when dealing with other countries.
79. Ibid., 88.
80. I see two possible counterarguments to this claim: (1) I have not pushed the Church-State synthesis as far as possible and that an overview of Christian Reconstructionism is necessary and (2) I have not taken a complete rejection of the world seriously, as in the Amish strain of Mennonites. I reply (1) Reconstructionism dismisses liberal democratic norms, even in non-exceptional times. Nothing in the Augustinian or Hauerwasian systems requires an outright rejection of liberal norms and (2) it is nearly impossible to study a negation, as the Amish do not interact with liberal thought. Hauerwas may reject liberalism as a basis of thought, but he operates within and attempts to communicate with liberal society. On Christian Reconstructionism, and its founder R. J. Rushdoony, see Michael Joseph McVicar, *Christian Reconstruction: R. J. Rushdoony and American Religious Conservatism* (Chapel Hill, NC: The University of North Carolina Press, 2015).

# 6

## Resting from Coercion

This conclusion will give a brief recap of my arguments and will contain an extended comment on Weber's bleak outlook for the future and whether the Christian tradition has the resources to face it. I will also return to medical metaphors through the Church as an antibody.

Given the Brexit vote in Great Britain, the earlier Scottish independence vote, the tensions in the Catalonia region of Spain, and the protestors in Hong Kong against the mainland government, it is clear that the concept of sovereignty has not been relegated to the dustbin of history quite yet. Sovereignty movements, especially in the form of populism, have swept through many liberal democracies. These movements are focused on the economic aspect of their respective countries. Lacking even the illusion of control over their own fates, these populations have latched onto figures who promise a return to "the good old days"[1] or "paleoliberalism."[2]

Weber suggests that such a return is not only improbable but likely impossible. In chapter 1, I detailed the debate in Weberian scholarship as to whether he should be read pessimistically or optimistically toward the future. I hinted that the pessimistic was the more likely option. But how does he explain his outlook, and if he is correct, what is the problem? One aspect of Weber's concern is societies' inability to return to pre-rationalization forms of being. Or as Weber puts it, "Wherever the modern specialized official comes to predominate, his power proves practically indestructible since the whole organization of even the most elementary want satisfaction has been tailored to his mode of operation."[3] Certainly, this is true of the bureaucratic nature of neoliberalism. Basic needs have been absorbed by the dictates of neoliberalism, making it cheaper to buy and ship products from the other side of the world than to make them in our own backyard. Efficiency has been the word of the millennium, whether in warfare (what is the minimum troop number necessary to secure Afghanistan?) or government bailouts.[4] The bureaucratization of non-economic forms of life, or the economization of all aspects of life, continues apace. Consider the following from Weber:

> An inanimate machine is mind objectified. Only this provides it with the power to force men into its service and to dominate their everyday working life as completely as is actually the case in the factory. Objectified intelligence is also that animated machine, the bureaucratic organization, with its specialization of trained skills, its division of jurisdiction, its rules and hierarchical relations of authority. Together with the inanimate machine it is busy fabricating the shell of bondage which men will perhaps be forced to inhabit some day, as powerless as the fellahs of ancient Egypt. This might happen *if* a technically superior administration *were to be the ultimate and sole value* in the ordering of their affairs, and that means: a rational bureaucratic administration with the corresponding welfare benefits, for this bureaucracy can accomplish much better than any other structure of domination.[5]

The transition from a manufacturing economy to a service-based economy does not undo Weber's worries. In fact, this transition may be more damaging, as the move to neoliberal globalization, which decimated the American working class, has created a chasm between the lower class and middle class. The totality of the factory (Weber's "inanimate machine") has merely taken on new forms in a non-manufacturing economy. The average worker in financial services or investments is just as dominated by their work as the late nineteenth/early twentieth-century factory worker was, but mentally instead of physically. The bondage to the machine of efficiency and better/faster/stronger mindset has not vanished with the factories of yesteryear. It has spread into every aspect of life in democratic societies. The major labor reforms, such as the forty-hour workweek, safety improvements, and so on, are not applicable to those who do not "labor" in similar ways.[6]

Weber's concerns with the future seems like a good place to begin the application of Christian ethics to the various problems I have diagnosed. The eschatological outlook of the early Church morphed into the Constantinian/Two Swords model which allowed for a level of cooperation between Church and Empire. That model was undermined by the Protestant Reformation, briefly allowing for the doctrine of *cuius regio eius religio* ("whose realm, his religion") which was an attempt to hold together the Church/State relationship. The Enlightenment was the final fracture between *regnum* and *sacerdotium* synthesis as "religion" was relegated to the private sphere of one's conscience. The twentieth century witnessed the failure of the State ideologies which had replaced public religion.[7] And though religion had regained some of its former footing (though not always in positive ways), it was economics, in the form of neoliberalism, which moved into the space emptied by the battle between capitalism and communism.

For Weber, however, history had already ended. Fukuyama's regularly misunderstood title was not referring to "events" but to "ideological evolution" in the form of the triumph of liberal democracy over other alternatives, namely "hereditary monarchy, fascism, and most recently communism."[8] In Fukuyama's own words:

> I argued that liberal democracy may constitute the "end point of mankind's ideological evolution" and the "final form of human government," and as such constituted the "end of history." That is, while earlier forms of government were characterized by grave defects and *irrationalities* that led to their eventual collapse, liberal democracy was arguably free from such fundamental internal contradictions.[9]

Weber had already seen the end of irrationalities in political systems. Fukuyama's argument is more at home in late nineteenth-century Germany than in the late twentieth-century world. The bureaucratic state was at home in either democratic or socialist systems.

> A progressive elimination of private capitalism is theoretically conceivable. . . . What would be the practical result? The destruction of the steel frame of modern industrial work? No! The abolition of private capitalism would simply mean that also the *top management* of the nationalized or socialized enterprises would become bureaucratic. Are the daily working conditions of the salaried employees and the workers in the state-owned Prussian mines and railroads really perceptibly different from those in big business enterprises? It is true that there is even less freedom, since every power struggle with a state bureaucracy is hopeless and since there is no appeal to an agency which as a matter of principle would be interested in limiting the employer's power, such as there is in the case of a private enterprise. *That* would be the whole difference.[10]

The bureaucratic State is the final evolution of human political progress because of its grounding as a rational exercise. The form of the State (liberal democratic, socialist, communist, fascist, etc.) is merely the first principle, the philosophical foundation upon which the rational, bureaucratic process builds. If there are built-in irrationalities to the form (as Fukuyama suggests with failed polities), a truly bureaucratic state would identify those irrationalities and transform the system as necessary to undo the irrational aspect. Perhaps it would be more appropriate to say that liberal democracy did not triumph over other political systems; the irrationalities inherent to the other systems were corrected, and the entire structure came down.[11]

By way of finishing my discussion of Weber, I want to make a comment on the spread or transmission of the bureaucratic mindset into different areas and why it seems so benign. The first deals with individualism as the basis of action. Because the "I" is at the center of Western life, the "I" demands that its time and energies are the most important. Impatience has elevated efficiency to the level of virtue. The most efficient companies are the most profitable ones. It is difficult to explain the rise and dominance of Amazon without understanding the bureaucratic rationalization of efficiency. Both the ordering and delivery process require the least amount of work at the highest speeds. This makes the shopping malls of only twenty years ago look like a baby-crawl race compared to the IndyCar speeds of Amazon. It is faster, cheaper, easier, and more environment-friendly to order online than to drive to the mall, look for parking, get to the store only to find out the product is out of stock, to then drive back home empty-handed. The unfortunate side effect of this is that American society has filled the saved time, money, and ease back into other consumerist pursuits. The "freedom" of time promised by efficiency is spent on another less-than-noble endeavor. It is a broader conception of freedom that moves Weber's concerns about the status of humanity in an increasingly bureaucratized world. The political life of Western societies is no longer focused on the common good, but on the efficient good. Candidates for political office are not judged on their policy positions but in relation to whom the party thinks can beat the rival candidate. Such power discourses are more at home in Foucault's thinking than Weber's and even more removed from the historic Christian teachings on the purpose of politics.

## REASSESSING CHRISTIAN ETHICS

Of course, the relationship between the Church and State is a complicated one. Jefferson's "wall of separation" was designed to keep the State out of the Church just as much as to keep the Church out of the State. Post-Enlightenment thought has maintained this separation as one of the key building blocks of civil society as the best way to protect liberty.

Natural antibodies destroy foreign material in the host's various bodily systems. The human body naturally "knows" which defensive mechanism to trigger. A cut finger does not trigger vomiting, likewise, an upset stomach does not force extra red blood cells to the fingers. As all metaphors do at some point, this one collapses in the reality that the Church has been less than stellar in knowing how to approach the problems of society, occasionally making the underlying condition even worse. The reality is that the Church as an institution is not a "natural" antibody. Instead, the Church is created, called out, assembled.[12] If I can stretch the metaphor once more, under this interpretation the Church is the vaccine for civil society, "repurposed" individuals who energize the natural antibodies.[13]

Patience is one of the "fruits of the Spirit," and rejecting the hyper-consumerism of modern society, whether in the pursuit of wealth or stuff, is commanded by Jesus in various passages of the gospels to his first-century context. And yet it seems wrong to claim that inefficiency should become a virtue even if efficiency carries a notion of impatience. *The Protestant Ethic and the Spirit of Capitalism* is not only about the problem of predestination but also about the valorization of work and working "as for the Lord rather than for men."[14] Purposeful inefficiency would seem to go against this admonition (even more so in the context of ancient slaves, to whom Paul addresses this part of the household code). If inefficiency is not the solution, is there another Christian virtue or practice that may help to inculcate a differing counter-dominant way of being?

The practice of refraining from work, as on the Jewish Sabbath, is one of the clearest areas for more exploration. One of Jesus's main criticisms of his Jewish interlocutors was their misunderstanding of the Sabbath. American Christians of all types, but especially Evangelicals, are in a similar situation. When the sermon ends, the local restaurants fill up, and an army of cooks, servers, and cleaners go to work. The commands to the ancient Israelites concerning the Sabbath were not specified to only the people of God. Since the shortening of the Ten Commandments into simple commands removes some critical context, the full command reads:

> Remember the sabbath day, to keep it holy. Six days you shall labor and do all your work, but the seventh day is a sabbath of the LORD your God; *in it* you shall not do any work, you or your son or your daughter, your male or your female servant or your cattle or your sojourner who stays with you.[15]

Every aspect of the ancient Israeli "economy" (understanding the anachronistic character of the word in this context) came to a standstill. But it was not merely rest for the Israelites; the sojourner (foreigner) was also forbidden from working. Christian sabbath notions which are *only* individually focused miss the communal character of the resting. Christians are no longer in a place of societal dominance that towns shut down on Sundays, nor do they have the power to enforce the legalism of so-called Blue Laws. This requires that "sabbath-rest" be applied by an individual to her context but in the community of the Church, blending the individualist and corporatist strains.

## BARTH AND FRANCIS

What would a sabbath-based narrative of humanity opposed to the neoliberal and bureaucratic rationality of society-at-large look like? I suggest that Karl

Barth's development of the Sabbath in *Church Dogmatics* and Pope Francis's remarks in *Evangelii Gaudium* are fruitful areas.

The Swiss-born Karl Barth is regarded as one (if not the) most important theologian of the twentieth century. Undoubtedly, part of his importance is his magnum opus, *Church Dogmatics*. However, his "arrival" on the theological scene was his *Römerbrief*, a commentary on Paul's Epistle to the Romans. Barth's concern in both works can be seen in the following passage:

> It is not man who brings the history of creation to an end, nor is it he who ushers in the subsequent history. It is God's rest which is the conclusion of the one and the beginning of the other, i.e., God's free, solemn, and joyful satisfaction with that which has taken place and has been completed as creation, and His invitation to man to rest with Him, i.e., with Him to be satisfied with that which has taken place through Him.[16]

This sums up the major themes of Barth's entire project: the freedom of God and the revelation of God to humanity to participate in the divine life. Part of that participation is in resting as the first "act" of God for which humanity was present was the resting on the seventh day.[17] According to Barth, God's rest shows both divine freedom and divine love.

> A world-principle without this limit [resting, or ending the creation process] to its creative activity would not be loving like God, but would be a being without love, never ceasing, never finding time for any creature, never satisfied with any, always positing other being in infinite sequence. Although it might seem to be an ocean of love, it would not really be love at all. Missing every possible object of love, at bottom it would be condemned to pursue its own shadow.[18]

Could we say the same of an economic system which never ceases, nor is satisfied, nor allows those participating in it to achieve either of these? The *telos* inherent in the seventh day is utterly alien to the neoliberal *telos*, which can never be achieved as a continuation is its "own shadow."[19] In fact, all economic (and social, and political) structures are never satisfied because they have become idols. Barth expands the understanding of "idols" from finite things, whether crafted material or the deification of animals or other perishable life, into the realm of "half-spiritual, half-material creations" namely "Family, Nation, State, Church, Fatherland."[20] Barth continues, "And so the 'No-God' is set up, idols are erected, and God, who dwells beyond all this and that, is 'given up.'"[21]

Barth argues that in the rejection of God, humanity is allowed to suffer the negative consequences of their idolatry. J. Kameron Carter highlights aspects of the following passage, stating, "As Barth insightfully understood, the image operating as the ideal—that is, as the Beautiful and thus as the master over the grotesque, to put it in aesthetic terms—is tied to the making of a slave."[22]

> The confusion avenges itself and becomes its own punishment. The forgetting of the true God is already itself the breaking loose of His wrath against those who forget Him. . . . The enterprise of setting up the "No-God" is avenged by its success. . . . Our conduct becomes governed precisely by what we desire. By a strict inevitability we reach the goal we have set before us. The images and likenesses, whose meaning we have failed to perceive, become themselves purpose and content and end. And now men have really become slaves and puppets of things, of "Nature" and of "Civilization", whose dissolution and establishing by God they have overlooked. And now there is no higher power to protect them from what they have set on high. . . . The whole ignominy of the course of the world they must now bear and bemoan and curse as ignominy; further, in their separation from God they must continue to give it ever new birth. They have wished to experience the known god of this world: well! they have experienced him.[23]

Thus, an economic or political system which sets up a "No-God" is doomed to a cyclical state of birth, death, re-birth, re-death. Humanity is forced to rely on the "No-God" for protection, as the true God has let them suffer the fate they have chosen. It should not surprise us that the worst of the effects of the apparent *deus absconditus* would fall on those which the system pushes to the margins. But this nihilism does not win the day.[24] The Christian tradition claims that God is the God of history and works through that history. Because of the Incarnation, we should see human actions (practices) and mindsets (values) which point to the "Yes-God" and the transformation of humanity out of the idolatry of the "No-God" of the world.

With the background of Barth's ideas, we can return to the issue of Sabbath-rest. The Old Testament requires that we take account of the Sabbath and Jubilee years.[25] Many scholars do not believe these commands were followed with any regularity.[26] Nevertheless, they have attracted a good deal of attention from different directions. Barth calls the Jubilee year "the *locus classicus* for theological opponents of the doctrine of free economy."[27] More recently, these commands have been applied to environmental[28] and animal ethics.[29] These applications are not entirely misplaced, but once again represent a symptomatic, not causal, approach to the problem.

A fully Christian ethic of Sabbath-rest must incorporate the implications of Jesus's many debates with the Pharisees over the interpretation of the Sabbath laws. The Gospels present two sources of controversy: picking grain to eat and healing.[30] Both suggest a wholeness or completeness of humanity;

a fulfillment of needs and a restoration of being. While both are physical, the latter has more connections to spiritual concepts. This double meaning is best seen in the Marcan telling: "And He said to them, 'Is it lawful to do good or to do harm on the Sabbath, to save a life or to kill?' But they kept silent."[31] The Greek word for "save" which is a clear reference to an act of healing in this context is *sōsai* from the root *sōdzo*. This is the same root that appears in Gabriel's annunciation of Jesus to Joseph: "and you shall call His name Jesus, for He will save His people from their sins."[32] The concept of the Great Physician, along with a motif of forgiveness of sins being an act of healing the individual (seen most clearly in the early understandings of the Eastern Church), comes from this shared etymological range.[33] The logic of Jesus's argumentation with the Pharisees is an ancient Semitic formula of *if x how much more y*, which occurs frequently in the Gospels.[34] Thus, Jesus is arguing, "If you will save your ox on the Sabbath, how much more will God attempt to save sick and hurting humans?"

Barth's understanding of Sabbath must be slightly altered to adequately address the Gospel testimony, as he limits his discussions of Sabbath to the Old Testament.[35] If the seventh day is God's free choice of rest and completion, then we must also accept that God has the freedom (a key motif in Barth) to define that rest in ways that may go against normal human conceptions. The free act of God's salvific power, whether physical or spiritual, is part of that completion of creation. Under this definition, Sabbath-rest is a call to participate in salvation, not a call to take a break.[36]

On the contemporary side, much of the work done in the area of Christian economics comes from Catholic thinkers who, due to the century-plus development of Catholic Social Teaching (CST), have a leg up on the Protestant traditions.[37] The grounding document of CST is Leo XIII's *Rerum Novarum*, which addressed the labor/capital conflicts at the end of the nineteenth century. Francis's *Evangelii Gaudium* is not a part of the *Rerum Novarum* tradition as it is focused on the missionary practices of the Church, not the Church's teaching on the proper ordering of society. However, Francis does draw on the CST tradition in his overview of the societal problems which the Church must wrestle within its evangelization attempts. He makes several comments on the economic aspect of contemporary society.

> One cause of this situation [the plight of the poor and the uncaring attitude towards them] is found in our relationship with money, since we calmly accept its dominion over ourselves and our societies. The current financial crisis can make us overlook the fact that it originated in a profound human crisis: the denial of the primacy of the human person! We have created new idols. The worship of the ancient golden calf (cf. *Ex* 32:1-35) has returned in a new and ruthless guise in the idolatry of money and the dictatorship of an impersonal

economy lacking a truly human purpose. The worldwide crisis affecting finance and the economy lays bare their imbalances and, above all, their lack of real concern for human beings; man is reduced to one of his needs alone: consumption.[38]

Here, Francis is pointing toward a theo-political issue at the heart of neoliberalism. Efficiency, low prices, free trade, are not goods in themselves. Instead, they are goods only for some other purpose. In the Augustinian-Thomistic tradition, any lesser good that is elevated to the highest good is a sign of idolatry (hence the reference to the Golden Calf), as only God is the highest good and is the end goal or *telos* of all humans. When one's vision is distracted through temptation (Genesis 3:6) or fear (Matthew 14:28-31) one's *telos* becomes obscured. Neoliberalism reframes humanity's *telos* in the pursuit of cheaper and faster consumption of goods. Ultimately, this misguided *telos* works backward, going beyond low prices, into a realm of dangerous moral outcomes:

> Human beings are themselves considered consumer goods to be used and then discarded. We have created a "throw away" culture which is now spreading. It is no longer simply about exploitation and oppression, but something new. Exclusion ultimately has to do with what it means to be a part of the society in which we live; those excluded are no longer society's underside or its fringes or its disenfranchised—they are no longer even a part of it. The excluded are not the "exploited" but the outcast, the "leftovers."[39]

The "excluded" are understood in different yet overlapping ways by a myriad of theories: subaltern studies, critical race theory, feminist theory, and postcolonial theory. Each of these theories would place the emphasis on a differing key aspect. Unfortunately, this is not the place to examine the intricacies and subtleties of each theory's impact on the nature of bureaucratic state power. Such discussions must be left for the future.

## PRACTICING ETHICS

As no ethical theory exists apart from real-world application, it is necessary to present a possible practice or discipline from within the Christian tradition that can adequately meet the needs that the theory identifies. There are two ways for Christian disciplines to manifest: inward virtue cultivation and/or outward signs of loving one's neighbor. The aforementioned Sabbath practice as participation in God's rest is an inward-facing practice. It may be that rest is "salvation" or "healing" in the case of the overworked single parent. It can also be the case that detaching one's sense of being from how Wall Street performed is also salvific in that it is a rejection (or at least the beginning of a rejection) from Barth's "No-God."

But if the Sabbath practice is an inner virtue, is there an outward-facing practice that supplements in as an expression of loving one's neighbor? I suggest that there is a dual-facing practice: Lent. The practice of Lent has been re-appropriated by some Protestant groups, Evangelicals in particular, as an important liturgical period and practice.[40] If the Sabbath is participation in the divine life through rest, Lent is participation in the divine life through self-denial. Such self-denial would be a necessary component for the developed world to fight against the self-gratification promised by neoliberalism.

Here we see the (apparent) paradox at the center of Christian ethics.[41] Self-gratification and self-denial are both necessary to counter the power of neoliberalism. The answer to the larger problem of bureaucracy, when answered from a Christian perspective, is both efficiency and inefficiency, both rationality and irrationality. I am not an expert on practical Christian theology and am therefore unable to describe what specific types of practices and disciplines would achieve this both/and paradox, but there is at least one possible candidate in the business world.[42]

If we were to apply this "paradoxical ethic" to the problem of sovereignty, in that both a defense and a rejection of one's political power were necessary, we begin to see how the democratic spirit has survived for so long. Democracy may be deeply flawed and based on a number of problematic premises, but acting in a democratic spirit (i.e., holding to an ideal-type of democracy in the face of its problems) is an act of political responsibility. The ideal is such that it captures the attention and imagination of the democrat to work toward it, even if the contradictions within its actual application may never be overcome. Coercion, albeit differently, cannot be out-coerced. The paradoxical ethic would lean toward a willful acceptance of the State's coercive power while fighting that power in areas in which it is applied unjustly. This would reconcile Romans 13 and Revelation 13 while containing the already/not-yet paradox of the Christian message. God is redeeming the world, including the political sphere, but the work is not finished. Unlike the social gospel proponents, this theory does not claim that humanity is to finish the work. Instead, Christians are called to participate in the divine work when and where possible. This is the greatest paradoxical ethic in the Christian ethical tradition: the Sovereign God has chosen to act through humanity in its weakness and frailness. This is not merely the most basic Christian teaching on the Incarnation. At its core, the story of *Heilsgeschichte* ("salvation history") in both the Jewish and Christian traditions is the story of human frailty and mistakes carrying along with God's plans even against the plans of the human actors making the decisions.

It may be that there is no way to integrate a paradoxical ethic into the bureaucracy, given the overriding impulse in such systems to lean toward one of the paradox's poles. It may be that Weber's pessimism of his future world is the realism of ours. The paradox ethic would require optimism and hope in the face of the iron cage. Such optimism may be unfounded, and such hope a fool's hope. Yet it would embrace the eschatological ethics found in the already/not-yet paradox of Pauline theology.[43] Such seemingly irrational hope would certainly conflict with the rational realism of the bureaucratic State. It is here we return to a redeemed Scrooge, a true Ebenezer,[44] who has rediscovered the joy of helping others and not forcing every aspect of his life in the pursuit of wealth. Yet even with Scrooge's wealth, there was only so much he could do against the poverty and need of his London.[45] Such an individual effort at the lowest level possible may be the only way to stand against the misuse of power by the coercive State. A re-enchantment of the world may be an impossibility, but a re-enchantment of ordinary lives may be within reach.

## NOTES

1. No matter what else is attached to the Trumpian slogan "Make America Great Again," a degree of nostalgia is a necessary part.

2. For a simplistic definition of "paleoliberalism," see Matthew Yglesias, "Hillary Clinton's Economic Policies Will Be to the Left of Obama's—or Bill Clinton's," vox.com, July 13, 2015, https://www.vox.com/2015/7/13/8940221/neo-paleo-liberalism. This would take a form similar to that of the late 1940s through the early 1970s in the American context, sometimes referred to as the "Old Left" in opposition to the "New Left" which is the precursor to the modern progressive movement. A full return is likely impossible; beyond the issues of globalization, the weakness of labor as an economic-political force (one of the key components of "Old Left" liberalism) seems unlikely to return to pre-1980s levels. Also of note, Yglesias's definition of neoliberalism is overly simplified and as expressed through the Democratic Party and its balancing of coalitions.

3. Weber, *ES*, 1401.

4. A company "too big to fail" is one that will distort the global market upon its collapse. It is more efficient to save the company than to let it fail and wait for a new iteration (through "normal" invisible hand market systems) to take its place.

5. Weber, *ES*, 1402. Emphasis original. The use of "welfare" should not be confused with the later phenomenon described by Wacquant.

6. While the majority of male suicides in America are members of physical labor industries, the second-highest subgroup is musicians and artists, the latter of which is also the highest subgroup for female suicides. The correlation I am drawing is that the most competitive sector of the service/entertainment industry is little better on the mental health of its workers than stereotypical blue-collar jobs. See Cora Peterson et

al., "Suicide Rates by Industry and Occupation—National Violent Death Reporting System, 32 States," *Morbidity and Mortality Weekly Report*, January 24, 2020, http://dx.doi.org/10.15585/mmwr.mm6903a1.

7. Robert Bellah's work on what he calls "civic religion" still stands as one of the most important works on the function of post-Enlightenment State ideologies/religions; see Robert N. Bellah, "Civil Religion in America," *Daedalus* 96, no. 1 (1967): 1–21, which set the stage for his later work on the topic.

8. Francis Fukuyama, *The End of History and the Last Man* (New York, NY: The Free Press, 1992), xi.

9. Ibid. Emphasis mine.

10. Weber, *E&S*, 1401–1402. Emphasis original.

11. This interpretation works best for the USSR and its client states, most notably East Germany. The one system that did not purge its irrationalities was fascism. This is one victory that liberal democracy can claim through its own force of will.

12. The Greek *ekklesia*, from which English has ecclesial and its cognates, can have both meanings.

13. The continuation of this metaphor is not immune from its previously mentioned issues. According to Protestant theology, there is no "natural" antibody in society to be activated due to Original Sin. Catholic theology has a bit more room for the metaphor with a differing emphasis on Original Sin. Finally, the vaccine metaphor breaks down in that vaccines use minimal or dead cells of the actual virus to stimulate the immune system. At an extremely far stretch, one could argue that the "baptism into death" (Romans 6:4) keeps the metaphor working. See Douglas Moo, *The Epistle to the Romans*, New International Commentary on the New Testament (Grand Rapids, MI: Eerdmans Publishing, 1996), 361–367 for an overview of the interpretative possibilities.

14. Colossians 3:23.

15. Exodus 20:8-10. The NASB uses italics to indicate implied words contained within grammatical structures or verb components.

16. Karl Barth, *Church Dogmatics*, ed. G. W. Bromiley and T. F. Torrance, trans. J. W. Edwards, O. Bussey, and H. Knight, 4 volumes (Peabody, MA: Hendrickson Publishers, 1958), 98. Hereinafter *CD*.

17. The creation account in Genesis does not have to be read literally for the underlying notion, the importance of rest, to remain. See Barth, III.1, ix–x, for his comments on science and the creation narrative.

18. Barth, *CD* III.1, 215.

19. Ibid., 215–228.

20. Karl Barth, *The Epistle to the Romans*, trans. Edwyn C. Hoskyns from the 6th German ed. (London: Oxford University Press, 1968), 50. Hereinafter *ER*.

21. Ibid., 50–51.

22. J. Kameron Carter, "Between W. E. B. Du Bois and Karl Barth: The Problem of Modern Political Theology," in *Race and Political Theology*, ed. Vincent W. Lloyd (Stanford, CA: Stanford University Press, 2012), 97.

23. Barth, *ER*, 51.

24. Romans 7, especially vv. 24-25.

25. Leviticus 25:1-55.

26. Barth, *CD* III.2, 457; Gordon J. Wenham, *The Book of Leviticus*, The New International Commentary on the Old Testament (Grand Rapids, MI: William B. Eerdmans Publishing Co., 1979), 318.

27. Ibid., 456.

28. Kathryn M. Schifferdecker, "Sabbath and Creation," *Word & World* 36, no. 3 (2016): 209–218; David Lazonby, "Applying the Jubilee to Contemporary Socio-Economic and Environmental Issues," *Journal of European Baptist Studies* 16, no. 3 (May 2016): 30–50.

29. A. Rahel Schafer, "Rest for the Animals?: Nonhuman Sabbath Repose in Pentateuchal Law," *Bulletin for Biblical Research* 23, no. 2 (2013): 167–186, especially note 6 which details the state of "biblical" animal ethics.

30. The issue of picking grain is a Synoptic feature (Matthew 12:1-8, Mark 2:23-8, Luke 6:1-5); healing on the Sabbath occurs in all four Gospels (Matthew 12:10-3, Mark 3:2-5, Luke 6:6-9 all detail the same incident; Luke 10:13-6; John 5:2-17; John 9:2-16).

31. Mark 3:4.

32. Matthew 1:21.

33. This West/East divide is often couched in terms of guilt/infirmity which needs judicial/therapeutic care, respectively. See Randy L. Maddox, *Responsible Grace: John Wesley's Practical Theology* (Nashville, TN: Kingswood Books, 1994), 73–93.

34. This logical form is known as "*qal wayyomer* ('light and heavy') by the rabbis and in the western tradition *a minori ad maius* ('from the minor to the major')," Moo, 309. The Apostle Paul frequently used this logical construction as well.

35. When Barth does turn to the Sabbath-breaking narratives in the New Testament, it is never about the Sabbath per se, but about some aspect of Jesus's personality or supposed self-understanding. See Barth, *CD* IV.2, 173–179 (Jesus's views on the Sabbath express both a "passive conservativism" and a "breach[] of the prevailing religious or cultic order").

36. Barth admits that there are "humanitarian" reasons for such rest, but that it "cannot bear a genuine categorical character" apart from the theological aspects of rest-as-participation. Without this aspect, humanity is simply left to as we are simply "left to [our own] devices." See Barth, *CD* IV.3, 47–72, esp. 60–61.

37. For example, Kenneth R. Himes, "Consumerism and Christian Ethics," *Theological Studies* 68, no. 1 (March 2007): 132–153, who is Franciscan; Albino Barrera, *Market Complicity and Christian Ethics*, New Studies in Christian Ethics (Cambridge: Cambridge University Press, 2011), who is Dominican; António Azevedo, "Recognizing Consumerism as an 'Illness of an Empty Soul': A Catholic Morality Perspective," *Psychology & Marketing* 37, no. 2 (February 2020): 250–259.

38. Francis, "Evangelii Gaudium," November 24, 2013, ¶ 55.

39. Ibid., ¶ 53. The "throw away" culture is exemplified in Huxley's *Brave New World*. Francis is likely also alluding to (or at the least, borrowing from) the pro-life tradition as developed by Saint Pope John Paul II.

40. Re-appropriation seems like the best word to describe the situation, given the hostility by many of the early Reformers to the practice as non-biblical. See Calvin,

*Institutes of the Christian Religion*, IV, 12, 20. Even those Protestants and Evangelicals who do observe Lent do not follow the Roman Catholic or Eastern Orthodox teachings on Lent.

41. Chesterton notes, "whenever we feel there is something odd in Christian theology, we shall generally find that there is something odd in the truth," *Orthodoxy*, 150.

42. Matthew McCreary, "Chick-Fil-A Makes More Per Restaurant Than McDonald's, Starbucks and Subway Combined . . . and It's Closed on Sundays," *Entrepreneur*, September 25, 2018, https://www.entrepreneur.com/article/320615.

43. The already/not-yet theological element concerns the Pauline theological notion that the Kingdom of God is already present on Earth due to Christ's resurrection, but is not yet fully realized in history. See James D. G. Dunn, *The Theology of Paul the Apostle* (Grand Rapids, MI: Eerdmans Publishing, 2006), 465.

44. I Samuel 7:12, best translated as "a stone of help."

45. This is one aspect which *The Muppets Christmas Carol* fails to develop: Dickens's larger social commentary on the problems facing the working classes of Victorian London. *A Christmas Carol* is not only a story of Scrooge's redemption but also a call to deal with the social problems facing its contemporary society.

# Bibliography

Abdelal, Rawi. *Capital Rules: The Construction of Global Finance*. Cambridge, MA: Harvard University Press, 2009.

Agamben, Giorgio. *Homo Sacer: Sovereign Power and Bare Life*. Stanford, CA: Stanford University Press, 1998.

———. *The Kingdom and the Glory: For a Theological Genealogy of Economy and Government*. Translated by Lorenzo Chiesa and Matteo Mandarini. Stanford, CA: Stanford University Press, 2011.

American Law Institute. *Restatement of the Law, Second, Contracts*. Vol. 1. 3 vols. St. Paul, MN: American Law Institute Publishers, 1981.

Andone, Irina, and Beatrice Scheubel. "Once Bitten: New Evidence on the Link between IMF Conditionality and IMF Stigma." *European Central Bank Working Paper Series*, no. 2262 (April 12, 2019).

Aquinas, Thomas. *Commentary on Aristotle's Nicomachean Ethics*. Translated by C. J. Litzinger. Notre Dame, IN: Dumb Ox Books, 1993.

———. *Summa Theologica*. London: Burns Oates & Washbourne; Fathers of the English Dominican Province, 1912.

Arendt, Hannah. *The Origins of Totalitarianism*. New York: Houghton Mifflin Harcourt Publishing Co., 1948.

Aristotle. *Nichomedean Ethics*. Translated by J. A. K. Thompson. New York: Penguin Books, 1976.

Augustine. *Augustine: Political Writings*. Translated by E. M. Atkins and R. J. Dodaro. Cambridge: Cambridge University Press, n.d.

Barrera, Albino. *Economic Compulsion and Christian Ethics*. Cambridge: Cambridge University Press, 2005.

Bazzana, Giovanni B. *Kingdom of Bureaucracy: The Political Theology of Village Scribes in the Sayings Gospel Q*. Bibliotheca Ephemeridum Theologicarum Lovaniensium, CCLXXIV. Leuven, Belgium: Peeters, 2015.

Bento, António. "From the Medieval Church as a Mystical Body to the Modern State as a Mystical Person: Ernst Kantorowicz and Carl Schmitt." In *Political Theology in Medieval and Early Modern Europe: Discourses, Rites, and Representations*, edited by Montserrat Herrero, Jaume Aurell, and Angela C. Miceli Stout. Turnhout, Belgium: Brepols, 2017.

Berger, J. M. *Without Prejudice: What Sovereign Citizens Believe*. Washington, DC: George Washington Program on Extremism, June 2016. https://extremism.gwu.edu/sites/g/files/zaxdzs5746/files/downloads/JMB%20Sovereign%20Citizens.pdf.

Bernstein, Steven, and William D. Coleman. "Introduction: Autonomy, Legitimacy and Power in an Era of Globalization." In *Unsettled Legitimacy: Political Community, Power, and Authority in a Global Era*, edited by Steven Bernstein and William D. Coleman. Vancouver, BC: UBC Press, 2009.

Biden, Joe. "Remarks by President Biden in a CNN Town Hall with Don Lemon." *The White House*, July 22, 2021. https://www.whitehouse.gov/briefing-room/speeches-remarks/2021/07/22/remarks-by-president-biden-in-a-cnn-town-hall-with-don-lemon/.

Bird, Brad. *The Incredibles*. Disney/Pixar, 2004.

Bourdieu, Pierre. *Acts of Resistance: Against the Tyranny of the Market*. Translated by Richard Nice. New York: The New Press, 1998.

———. "Rethinking the State: The Genesis and Structure of the Bureaucratic Field." Translated by Loïc J. D. Wacquant and Samar Farage, *Sociological Theory* 12, no. 1 (1994): 1–18.

———. "The Abdication of the State." In *The Weight of the World*, translated by Priscilla Parkhurst Ferguson. Stanford, CA: Stanford University Press, 1999.

Brooks, David. "Obama, Gospel and Verse." *The New York Times*, April 26, 2007. http://www.nytimes.com/2007/04/26/opinion/26brooks.html.

Brown, Peter. *Augustine of Hippo*. Oakland, CA: University of California Press, 2000.

Brown, Wendy. *Undoing the Demos: Neolberalism's Stealth Revolution*. New York: Zone Books, 2015.

Brueggemann, Walter. *Old Testament Theology: An Introduction*. Nashville, TN: Abingdon Press, 2008.

Burleigh, Michael. *Earthly Powers: The Clash of Religion and Politics from the French Revolution to the Great War*. New York: HarperCollins, 2005.

Cahill, Lisa Sowle. "Sovereign No More? Selves, States, and God in Our Bewildering Global Environment." In *Jean Bethke Elshtain: Politics, Ethics, and Society*, edited by Debra Erickson and Michael Le Chevallier. Notre Dame, IN: Notre Dame University Press, 2018.

Calvin, John. *Commentaries on the Four Last Books of Moses Arranged in the Form of a Harmony*. Edinburgh: Calvin Translation Society, 1852.

———. *Institutes of the Christian Religion*. Translated by Henry Beveridge. Bellingham, WA: Logos Bible Software, 1997.

Carson, E. Ann, and Rich Kluckow. "Prisoners in 2022 – Statistical Tables." *Bureau of Justice Statistics*, November 2023.

Chesterton, Gilbert K. *Orthodoxy*. New York: John Lane Company, 1908.

Coicaud, Jean-Marc. *Legitimacy and Politics: A Contribution to the Study of Political Right and Political Responsibility*. Translated by David Ames Curtis. Cambridge: Cambridge University Press, 2002.

Communications Act of 1934 (amended by Telecom Act of 1996), 47 U.S.C. § 230(c)(1).

Coronel, Sheila, Steve Coll, and Derek Kravitz. "Rolling Stone & UVA: Columbia School of Journalism's Report." *Rolling Stone* (blog), April 5, 2015. https://www.rollingstone.com/culture/culture-news/rolling-stone-and-uva-the-columbia-university-graduate-school-of-journalism-report-44930/.

Cotter, Padraig. "The Muppets Christmas Carol: Why 'When Love Is Gone' Is Missing in Some Cuts." *ScreenRant*. https://screenrant.com/muppets-christmas-carol-when-love-gone-cut-reason/ (Accessed March 5, 2020).

Dawson, Angus, and Marcel Verweij, eds. *Ethics, Prevention, and Public Health*. New York: Oxford University Press, 2007.

"'Disinformation Nation: Social Media's Role in Promoting Extremism and Misinformation.'" Washington, DC, March 25, 2021. https://www.congress.gov/event/117th-congress/house-event/111407/text.

Douglas, Mary. *Purity and Danger: An Analysis of Concepts of Pollution and Taboo*. New York: Routledge, 2002.

Doyle, Charles. *Federal Mandatory Minimum Sentencing Statutes*. Washington, DC: Congressional Research Service, September 9, 2013.

Dreher, Rod. *The Benedict Option: A Strategy for Christians in a Post-Christian Nation*. New York: Sentinel, 2017.

Dronberger, Ilse. *The Political Thought of Max Weber: In Quest of Statesmanship*. New York: Meredith Corp., 1971.

Dunn, James D. G. "Romans 13:1-7: A Charter for Political Quietism?" *Ex Auditu* 2 (1986): 55–68.

Durkheim, Émile. *The Elementary Forms of Religious Life*. Translated by Carol Cosman. New York: Oxford University Press, 2001.

Eichengreen, Barry, and Ngaire Woods. "The IMF's Unmet Challenges." *Journal of Economic Perspectives* 30, no. 1 (2016): 29–51.

Ellis, Barbara A., Drue H. Barrett, John D. Arras, and Bruce Jennings. "Introduction." In *Emergency Ethics: Public Health Preparedness and Response*. New York: Oxford University Press, 2016.

Elshtain, Jean Bethke. *Public Man, Private Woman: Women in Social and Political Thought*. Princeton, NJ: Princeton University Press, 1981.

———. *Sovereignty: God, State, and Self*. New York: Basic Books, 2008.

Finstuen, Andrew S. *Original Sin and Everyday Protestants: The Theology of Reinhold Niebuhr, Billy Graham, and Paul Tillich in an Age of Anxiety*. Chapel Hill, NC: The University of North Carolina Press, 2009.

Fitzmyer, Joseph A. *Romans: A New Translation with Introduction and Commentary*. New Haven, CT: Yale University Press, 1993.

Foucault, Michel. *Discipline and Punish: The Birth of the Prison*. New York: Vintage Books, 1995.

———. *The Birth of Biopolitics: Lectures at the College de France, 1978-79*. Edited by Michel Senellart. Translated by Graham Burchell. New York: Palgrave MacMillian, 2008.

Fuller, Lon. *Legal Fictions*. Stanford, CA: Stanford University Press, 1967.

Gardner, John. "The Many Faces of the Reasonable Person." *Law Quarterly Review*, no. 131 (2015): 563–584.

Gauchet, Marcel. *The Disenchantment of the World: A Political History of Religion*. Translated by Oscar Burge. Princeton, NJ: Princeton University Press, 1997.

Gillam, Terry, and Terry Jones. *Monty Python and the Holy Grail*. EMI Films, 1975.

Glassman, Ronald M., William H. Swatos Jr., and Paul L. Rosen, eds. *Bureaucracy Against Democracy and Socialism*. New York: Greenwood Press, 1987.

Goldberg, Jonah. *The Tyranny of Clichés: How Liberals Cheat in the War of Ideas*. New York: Sentinel, 2012.

Goosen, Rachel Waltner. "'Defanging the Beast': Mennonite Responses to John Howard Yoder's Sexual Abuse." *Mennonite Quarterly Review* 89 (January 2015): 7–80.

Gradel, Ittai. *Emperor Worship and Roman Religion*. New York: Oxford University Press, 2002.

Graeber, David. *Bullshit Jobs: A Theory*. New York: Simon & Schuster, 2019.

Gruber, Judith E. *Controlling Bureaucracies: Dilemmas in Democratic Governance*. Berkley, CA: University of California Press, 1987.

Gupta, Nijay K., and Fredrick J. Long. "The Politics of Ephesians and the Empire: Accommodation or Resistance." *Journal of Greco-Roman Christianity & Judaism* 7 (January 2010): 112–136.

Hamilton, Mary R. "Democracy and Public Service." In *Democracy in Public Administration*, edited by Richard C. Box. Armonk, NY: M.E. Sharpe, Inc., n.d.

Hauerwas, Stanely. *After Christendom?: How the Church Is to Behave If Freedom, Justice, and a Christian Nation Are Bad Ideas*. Nashville, TN: Abingdon Press, 1999.

———. "Speaking Christian: A Commencement Address for Eastern Mennonite Seminary." *Mennonite Quarterly Review* 84, no. 3 (July 2010): 41–49.

Hauerwas, Stanley, and William H. Willimon. *Resident Aliens*. Nashville, TN: Abingdon Press, 1989.

Hay, Colin. *Why We Hate Politics*. Cambridge, MA: Polity Press, 2007.

Henson, Brian. *The Muppet Christmas Carol*. Walt Disney Pictures, 1992.

Hobbes, Thomas. *Leviathan*. Edited by G. A. J. Rogers and Karl Schuhmann. London: Thoemmes Continuum, 2005.

Hutson, Christopher Roy. "Enough for What?: Playacting Isaiah 53 in Luke 22:35-38." *Restoration Quarterly* 55, no. 1 (2013): 35–51.

Igo, Sarah E. *The Known Citizen: A History of Privacy in Modern America*. Cambridge, MA: Harvard University Press, 2018.

Jennings, Bruce. "Public Health and Civic Republicanism: Toward an Alternative Framework for Public Health Ethics." In *Ethics, Prevention, and Public Health*, edited by Angus Dawson and Marcel Verweij. New York: Oxford University Press, 2007.

Johnston, Deborah, and Alfredo Saad-Filho. *Neoliberalism: A Critical Reader*. London: Pluto Press, 2005.

Kanno-Youngs, Zolan, and Cecilia Kang. "'They're Killing People': Biden Denounces Social Media for Virus Disinformation." *New York Times*, July 19, 2021.

Kirwan, Michael. *Political Theology: A New Introduction*. London: Darton, Longman and Todd, 2008.

Klauck, Hans-Josef. *The Religious Context of Early Christianity: A Guide to Graeco-Roman Religions*. Minneapolis, MN: Fortress Press, 2003.

Koester, Craig R. "The Number of the Beast in Revelation 13 in Light of Papyri, Graffiti, and Inscriptions." *Journal of Early Christian History* 6, no. 3 (2016): 1–21.

Kolla, Edward James. *Sovereignty, International Law, and the French Revolution*. New York: Cambridge University Press, 2017.

Koontz, Theodore J. "Christian Nonviolence: An Interpretation." In *Christian Political Ethics*, edited by John A. Coleman. Princeton, NJ: Princeton University Press, 2008.

Kotsko, Adam. *Neoliberalism's Demons: On the Political Theology of Late Capital*. Stanford, CA: Stanford University Press, 2018.

Kulldorff, Martin, Sunetra Gupta, and Jay Bhattacharya. "The Great Barrington Declaration," October 4, 2020. https://gbdeclaration.org/.

Leithart, Peter J. *Defending Constantine: The Twilight of an Empire and the Dawn of Christendom*. Downers Grove, IL: InterVarsity Press, 2010.

Lewis, C. S. *The Screwtape Letters*. Annotated. New York: HarperCollins, 2013.

Locke, John. *Two Treatises of Government: And a Letter Concerning Toleration*. Edited by Ian Shapiro. New Haven, CT: Yale University Press, 2003.

Macias, Amanda. "From Aruba to Iceland, These 36 Nations Have No Standing Military." *CNBC*, April 3, 2018. https://www.cnbc.com/2018/04/03/countries-that-do-not-have-a-standing-army-according-to-cia-world-factbook.html.

MacIntyre, Alasdair. *After Virtue*. 2nd ed. Notre Dame, IN: Notre Dame University Press, 1984.

———. *Whose Justice? Which Rationality?* Notre Dame, IN: Notre Dame University Press, 1988.

Magalhães, Pedro T. "A Contingent Affinity: Max Weber, Carl Schmitt, and the Challenge of Modern Politics." *Journal of the History of Ideas* 77, no. 2 (April 2016): 283–304.

Major, Aaron. *Architects of Austerity: International Finance and the Politics of Growth*. Stanford, CA: Stanford University Press, 2014.

Mazzei, Patricia, Frances Robles, and Maggie Astor. "Rick Scott Wins Florida Senate Recount as Bill Nelson Concedes." *New York Times*, November 28, 2018, sec. U.S.

McGregor, Joan. "Bargaining Advantages and Coercion in the Market." *Philosophy Research Archives* XIV (1989 1988): 23–50.

McVicar, Michael Joseph. *Christian Reconstruction: R. J. Rushdoony and American Religious Conservatism*. Chapel Hill, NC: The University of North Carolina Press, 2015.

Miller, William Robert. *Nonviolence: A Christian Interpretation*. New York: Association Press, 1964.

*Missouri v. Biden*, No. 3:22-CV-01213 (U.S. Dist. Ct. W. Dist. La. Monroe Div. July 4, 2023).

Mitchell, William, and Thomas Fazi. *Reclaiming the State: A Progressive Vision of Sovereignty for a Post-Neoliberal World*. London: Pluto Press, 2017.

Mitzman, Arthur. *The Iron Cage: An Historical Interpretation of Max Weber*. New York: Alfred A. Knopf, 1970.

Moltmann, Jürgen. *On Human Dignity: Political Theology and Human Rights*. Minneapolis, MN: Fortress Press, 1987.

*Murthy v. Missouri*, No. 23–411 (Supreme Court of the United States June 26, 2024).

National Intelligence Council. "Updated Assessment on COVID-19 Origins." Office of the Director of National Intelligence, October 29, 2021. https://www.dni.gov/files/ODNI/documents/assessments/Declassified-Assessment-on-COVID-19-Origins.pdf.

New York Times. "2016 Michigan Results." *New York Times*, August 1, 2017. https://www.nytimes.com/elections/2016/results/michigan.

Niebuhr, Reinhold. *Moral Man and Immoral Society: A Study in Ethics and Politics.* 2nd ed. Louisville, KY: John Knox Press, 2013.

Nisbet, Robert. *The Quest for Community: A Study in the Ethics of Order and Freedom.* Wilmington, DE: ISI Books, 2010.

O'Brien, Glen. "John Wesley's Rebuke to the Rebels of British America: Revisiting the Calm Address." *Methodist Review* 4 (2012): 31–55.

O'Donovan, Oliver. *The Desire of the Nations.* New York: Cambridge University Press, 1996.

Office of Family Assistance. "Characteristics and Financial Circumstances of TANF Recipients Fiscal Year (FY) 2022." *Department of Health and Human Services*, October 30, 2023.

Pew Research Center. "Americans' Trust in Scientists, Positive Views of Science Continue to Decline." November 2023.

Phillips, Elizabeth. *Political Theology: A Guide for the Perplexed.* New York: T&T Clark, 2012.

"President Biden White House Departure." *C-SPAN*, July 16, 2021. https://www.c-span.org/video/?513464-1/president-biden-white-house-departure.

Queally, James, Richard Winton, and Hailey Branson-Potts. "Weinstein Cites 'Casting Couch' Defense as He Faces Rape Charges in New York." *Latimes.Com*, May 26, 2018. http://www.latimes.com/local/lanow/la-me-ln-weinstein-case-20180526-story.html.

Reed, Isaac Ariail. "Power and the French Revolution." *Historicka Sociologie* 1 (2018): 47–70.

Rosenblatt, Helena. *Rousseau and Geneva: From the First Discourse to The Social Contract, 1749–1762.* Ideas in Context. Cambridge: Cambridge University Press, 1997.

Rothman, Robert. *Something in Common: The Common Core Standards and the Chapter in American Education.* Cambridge, MA: Harvard Education Press, 2011.

Rousseau, Jean-Jaques. *The Social Contract.* Edited by Maurice Cranston. New York: Penguin Books, 2006.

Ryder, Phyllis Mentzell. "In(Ter)Ventions of Global Democracy: An Analysis of the Rhetorics of the A-16 World Bank/IMF Protests in Washington, DC." *Rhetoric Review* 25, no. 4 (October 2006): 408–426.

Sabine, George H. *A History of Political Theory.* New York: Henry Holt and Company, 1937.

Sadurski, Wojciech. *Equality and Legitimacy.* New York: Oxford University Press, 2008.

Said, Edward. *Orientalism.* New York: Random House, 1978.

Scaff, Lawrence A. *Fleeing the Iron Cage: Culture, Politics, and Modernity in the Thought of Max Weber.* Berkley, CA: University of California Press, 1989.

Schmitt, Carl. *Political Theology: Four Chapters on the Concept of Sovereignty.* Translated by George Schwab. Cambridge, MA: The MIT Press, 1985.

Scott, Peter, and William T. Cavanaugh, eds. *The Blackwell Companion to Political Theology*. Malden, MA: Blackwell Publishing, 2004.
Sewell Jr., William H. *The Logics of History: Social Theory and Social Transformation*. Chicago, IL: University of Chicago Press, 2005.
Simmons, A. John. "Locke's State of Nature." In *The Social Contract Theorists: Critical Essays on Hobbes, Locke, and Rousseau*, edited by Christopher W. Morris. Critical Essays on the Classics. Lanham, MD: Rowman & Littlefield Publishers, 1999.
Slobodian, Quinn. *Globalists: The End of Empire and the Birth of Neoliberalism*. Cambridge, MA: Harvard University Press, 2018.
Smith, Lauren Edwards, Laura R. Olson, and Jeffery A. Fine. "Substantive Religious Representation in the U.S. Senate: Voting Alignment with the Family Research Council." *Political Research Quarterly* 63, no. 1 (March 2010): 68–82.
Smith, Thomas W. "Authority and Liberty: John Wesley's View of Medieval England." *Wesley and Methodist Studies* 7, no. 1 (2015): 1–26.
Søe, Sille Obelitz. "A Unified Account of Information, Misinformation, and Disinformation." *Synthese* 198, no. 6 (June 2021): 5929–5949.
Stapleford, John E. *Bulls, Bears and Golden Calves: Applying Christian Ethics in Economics*. 3rd ed. Downers Grove, IL: IVP Academic, 2015.
Stolberg, Sheryl Gay, Benjamin Mueller, and Carl Zimmer. "The Origins of the Covid Pandemic: What We Know and Don't Know." *New York Times*, March 17, 2023. https://www.nytimes.com/article/covid-origin-lab-leak-china.html.
Tax Policy Center. "What Are Marriage Penalties and Bonuses?" Accessed February 10, 2020. https://www.taxpolicycenter.org/briefing-book/what-are-marriage-penalties-and-bonuses.
Tilly, Charles. "War Making and State Making as Organized Crime." In *Bringing the State Back In*, edited by Peter B. Evans, Dietrich Rueschemeyer, and Theda Skocpol. Cambridge: Cambridge University Press, 1985.
Tobias, Jimmy. "Unredacted NIH Emails Show Efforts to Rule Out Lab Origin of Covid." *The Intercept*, January 19, 2023. https://theintercept.com/2023/01/19/covid-origin-nih-emails/.
*United States v. Carter*, No. 16-20032-02-JAR (Dist. Kan. January 25, 2019).
Vagins, Deborah J., and Jesselyn McCurdy. *Cracks in the System: Twenty Years of the Unjust Federal Crack Cocaine Law*. Washington, DC: The American Civil Liberties Union, 2006.
Verweij, Marcel, and Angus Dawson. "The Meaning of 'Public' in 'Public Health'." In *Ethics, Prevention, and Public Health*, edited by Angus Dawson and Marcel Verweij. New York: Oxford University Press, 2007.
Volokh, Alexander. "N Guilty Men." *University of Pennsylvania Law Review*, no. 1 (1997): 173–216.
Wacquant, Loïc. *Punishing the Poor: The Neoliberal Government of Social Insecurity*. Durham, NC: Duke University Press, 2009.
Weber, Max. *Economy and Society: An Outline of Interpretive Sociology*. Edited by Guenther Roth and Claus Wittich. Vol. 2. 2 vols. Berkley, CA: University of California Press, 1968.

———. "Politics as a Vocation." In *Max Weber's Complete Writings on Academic and Political Vocations*, edited by John Dreijmanis, translated by Gordon C. Wells. New York: Algora Publishing, 2008.

Weiss, Bari. "Guilty of Not Being a Mind Reader." *New York Times*, January 17, 2018.

Wenger, J. C., trans. "Schleitheim Confession of the Swiss Brethren." *Mennonite Quarterly Review* XIX, no. 4 (October 1945): 247–253.

Wertheimer, Alan. *Coercion*. Studies in Moral, Political, and Legal Philosophy. Princeton, NJ: Princeton University Press, 2014.

Wesley, John. *A Calm Address to Our American Colonies*. London: R. Hawes, 1775. https://archive.org/details/calmaddresstoour00wesl.

Whitehead, Alfred North. *Process and Reality: An Essay in Cosmology*. Edited by David Ray Griffin and Donald W. Sherburne. New York: Free Press, 1978.

Witherington, Ben, and Darlene Hyatt. *Paul's Letter to the Romans: A Socio-Rhetorical Commentary*. Grand Rapids, MI: Eerdmans Publishing, 2004.

Wood, Ellen Meiksins. *Liberty and Property: A Social History of Western Political Thought from Renaissance to Enlightenment*. New York, NY: Verso, 2012.

Woods, Ngaire. *The Globalizers: The IMF, the World Bank, and Their Borrowers*. Ithaca, NY: Cornell University Press, 2006.

Yerby, George. *People and Parliament: Representative Rights and the English Revolution*. New York, NY: Palgrave MacMillian, 2008.

Yoder, John Howard. *The Politics of Jesus: Vicit Agnus Noster*. 2nd ed. Grand Rapids, MI: William B. Eerdmans, 1994.

# Index

Agamben, Giorgio, 17, 39n81
American Constitution, 88–89
American Revolution, 1, 30
Aquinas, Thomas, 21, 54n5, 116–17, 119
Aristotle, 23, 41–42, 122
Augustine, 6, 114–16, 118–20, 127

Bourdieu, Pierre, 35, 59, 69–70, 82–83
bureaucracy, 4–5, 35, 65–71, 89–90; efficiency, 14, 62, 69–70, 76–78, 91, 94, 125–26, 137–38, 140

Calvin, John, 119–21
Charles I, 19, 23
Charles II, 14, 19, 70
coercion, 3–5, 10–11, 20, 22–23, 59–61, 64–65, 69–70, 75–82, 85, 89, 92, 96–98, 100–3, 115–18, 123, 126–27, 146–47; democracy, 47–53; legal, 41–47, 64–65; philosophical, 41–45
Constantine, 2, 123–24, 127, 138
COVID-19, 97–101. *See also* public health

drugs, 65, 90–91; war on, 2

European Union, 11n6, 25

Foucault, Michel, 59, 88, 92, 114; *Discipline and Punish*, 50–51; Panopticon, 15, 64, 91–92
French Revolution, 1, 15, 27, 30–31

Germany, 62, 68, 118, 139; Third Reich, 15, 118; Weimar Republic, 13–17
Gutiérrez, Gustavo, 6, 124

Hauerwas, Stanely, 109, 123–27, 130
Hitler, Adolf, 14–15, 17
Hobbes, Thomas, 10, 13, 18–29, 34, 48, 110, 122; *De cive*, 19; *Leviathan*, 19–23
Hume, David, 16, 69–70

Internal Revenue Service (IRS), 3–4, 64
International Monetary Fund (IMF), 79–81

liberalism, 67, 126; the People, 10, 13, 16, 32, 47, 52–53, 62, 66–67, 70, 71, 122. *See also* sovereignty, democratic
liberation theology, 3, 6–7
Locke, John, 13, 23–27
Luther, Martin, 7, 117–18

MacIntyre, Alisdair, 8–9, 17, 67–70, 94, 125
"Me Too" hashtag movement, 34, 46
Metz, Jean-Baptiste, 6–7
Moltmann, Jurgen, 6–7, 118

neoliberalism, 75–83, 96, 127, 137–39, 145–46
Niebuhr, Reinhold, 109, 128–29

Obama, Barack, 128
O'Donovan, Oliver, 9, 39n82

Paul, 61, 111–13, 116, 141–42, 147
political theology, 4, 6–7, 9
poverty, 85–87, 147; war on, 2
privacy, 87–90
public health, 96–97
public theology, 3, 6–7

Rousseau, Jean-Jaques, 27–30

Schmitt, Carl, 6–7, 13–18, 52–53, 71, 117, 122; Nazi Party, 15; *Political Theology*, 6, 15; state of exception, 16, 31–32, 34–35, 53–54, 66, 70–71, 81, 96
sovereign citizens, 88
sovereignty, 3–5, 8, 10, 13–20, 32–35, 41, 51–54, 59, 65–67, 70–71, 75, 81–82, 98–99, 101, 117, 122, 137; democratic, 31, 47–50, 52–53, 71, 129; God's, 8, 78, 110–12, 114, 120–21, 146

Supreme Court of the United States of America, 108n87
surveillance, 65, 83–84

technocrat, 66–67

United States of America: and 2016 elections, 1, 17; and 2020 elections, 1, 98; and 2024 elections, 1

Weber, Max, 13–17, 33–35, 59
welfare, 65, 84–88, 103
Wesley, John, 121–22
World Bank. *See* International Monetary Fund

Yoder, John Howard, 109, 123–24, 127–30

# About the Author

**Steven T. Lane** (PhD Religion, FSU) is a visiting teaching faculty at Florida State University in the Department of Religion. His research focuses on Christian Ethics and Political Thought. He and his wife have three children, two cats, a dog, and a bird.